Praise for *Bereshit*

"It is my sincere pleasure to endorse Ines Toto Furume's book titled *Bereshit: A Biblical Approach to Leadership*. Dr. Ines mines both the successes and failures of leaders in the Bible to draw out deep lessons for us to apply to our leadership. Starting in Genesis 1:1, she grounds leadership in the very character of God. I recommend this book to anyone who wants an overview of leadership in the Bible."

—W. David Winner, PhD
Adjunct Professor at Regent University

"The book entitled, *Bereshit: A Biblical Approach to Leadership*, is a very exciting and inspiring manuscript that has excellent, relevant application for Christian leaders and outstanding insights into what it means to succeed as a leader with a biblical worldview. This book has a solid biblical foundation to help leaders through their journey, much like your personal journey of trusting God and learning to overcome through His guidance. You have done especially well at writing this book from the perspective of a blend of your personal leadership experiences in the workplace and your new understanding from the DSL program with a solid scholarly voice. This blend helps Christian leaders relate well to the problems and issues of leading while being 'salt and light,' and it offers solid hands-on solutions and recommendations for best practices that are grounded in scripture and the literature. It has been my honor to work with you and pray that God would bless your efforts in writing and that it will be of great use in your ministry and career."

—Rob Freeborough, PhD, MBA, M.Div., SPHR
Faculty at Regent University

"Detailed. Enlightening. Scripturally based. Leadership-potential stirring. Balanced and practical. Simple; down to earth but powerful. These are few of the multiple words that have been springing up in my heart when going through this work. Ines has nailed it to what it should really be.

"In this part of the world, in Africa, we have, in fact, an ever-increasing number of graduates from great universities—just too much of politicians, just too many priests and pastors, just too much of title bearers—not to mention of natural resources—yet we are still in want of true leaders. This is a timely book! I would therefore strongly recommend this book to both aspiring and already operating leaders in any field. Congratulations, Ines Furume-Mangala!"

—Schekinah Masudi A.
Chancellor at VIP University

"Dr. Ines Toto Furume has created an outstanding resource that begins to show the influence that the Bible can have on our understanding of leadership. As well, and perhaps just as importantly, Dr. Furume shows how leadership can be pursued in a uniquely Christian manner that reflects Jesus. I wholeheartedly endorse her work to all aspiring Christian leaders."

—Russell L. Huizing, PhD
Adjunct Professor at Regent University

BERESHIT

BERESHIT

A Biblical Approach to Leadership

Dr. Ines Furume-Mangala

Although the author has made every effort to ensure that the information in this book was correct at the time of first publication, the author does not assume and hereby disclaims any liability to any party for any loss, damage, or disruption caused by errors or omissions, whether such errors or omissions result from negligence, accident, or any other cause.

Copyright © 2023 by Dr. Ines Furume-Mangala

All rights reserved. No part of this book may be reproduced or transmitted in any form or by any means, electronic or mechanical, including photocopying, recording, or any information storage and retrieval system, without permission in writing from the publisher. For more information, address BookLogix, c/o Permissions Department, 1264 Old Alpharetta Rd., Alpharetta, GA 30005.

ISBN: 978-1-6653-0466-5 - Paperback
eISBN: 978-1-6653-0467-2 - ePub

These ISBNs are the property of BookLogix for the express purpose of sales and distribution of this title. The content of this book is the property of the copyright holder only. BookLogix does not hold any ownership of the content of this book and is not liable in any way for the materials contained within. The views and opinions expressed in this book are the property of the Author/Copyright holder, and do not necessarily reflect those of BookLogix.

Library of Congress Control Number: 2023907110

♾This paper meets the requirements of ANSI/NISO Z39.48-1992 (Permanence of Paper)

Scripture quotations marked "NIV" are taken from the Holy Bible, New International Version®, NIV®. Copyright © 1973, 1978, 1984, 2011 by Biblica, Inc.™ Used by permission of Zondervan. All rights reserved worldwide. Scripture quotations marked "NLT" are taken from the Holy Bible, New Living Translation, copyright © 1996, 2004, 2007 by Tyndale House Foundation. Used by permission of Tyndale House Publishers, Inc., Carol Stream, Illinois 60188. All rights reserved. Scriptures marked as "GNT" are taken from the Good News Translation-Second Edition © 1992 by American Bible Society. Used by permission. Scripture quotations marked "ESV" are from the ESV® Bible (The Holy Bible, English Standard Version®), copyright © 2001 by Crossway, a publishing ministry of Good News Publishers. Used by permission. All rights reserved. Scripture quotations marked "KJV" are taken from the Holy Bible, King James Version (Public Domain). Scripture quotations marked "NASB" are taken from the New American Standard Bible®, Copyright © 1960, 1962, 1963, 1968, 1971, 1972, 1973, 1975, 1977, 1995 by The Lockman Foundation. Used by permission.

051023

This book is dedicated to all leaders, especially Christian leaders, who are trying to navigate their leadership journey based on biblical principles. Your desire to be Christ-like inspired me to write this manuscript.

Thank you for allowing me to be part of your journey through this book.

Contents

Foreword ix
Preface xi
Introduction xiii

Part One   Leadership Is   **1**

Chapter One
   What Is Leadership?   3
Chapter Two
   Leadership Is God-Ordained   9
Chapter Three
   Leadership Is a Mind-Set   17
Chapter Four
   Are Leaders Born or Made?   29

Part Two   How Some Leaders Succeeded   **35**

Introduction   37
Chapter Five
   Invest in the Vision and Mission   39
Chapter Six
   Invest in Effective Communication   45
Chapter Seven
   Building a Team   51
Chapter Eight
   Invest in Building Relationships: Build Trust   61

Part Three   How Some Leaders Failed   **71**

Chapter Nine
   Lack of Ethical Leadership   73
Chapter Ten
   Lack of Boundaries in Leadership   85

Part Four   Conclusion   **95**

Appendix
   A.   Self-Reflection Questionnaire   101
   B.   Must-Know Bible Verses for Leaders   102

References   103
Acknowledgments   109

Foreword

Every leader desires to do well, but not all leaders desire to lead with biblical foundations. Dr. Furume provides a unique perspective to show readers the "why" of why the Bible matters to today's leaders.

When Dr. Furume asked me to write the foreword, I happily agreed, but then stumbled, as I was not familiar with "Bereshit"—what is this new term? As an academic, it was exciting to learn how this is intended to take us back to the beginning. If you have ever journeyed back to your beginnings or the beginnings of anything, then you know this is where the foundation is! What you build on, where you start, the impetus, determines the strength we journey with, our foundation. Every Christian leader needs to ask what their source is, their foundation, their beginning.

For the reader of this book, I would encourage you to seek and ask about your own beginnings, your own foundation—knowing this will take you where you need to go. Ask yourself, why are you a leader? What is your leadership philosophy? Start at your beginning; let's build a foundation, a strong one. And what should be your foundation? As a Christian leader, it must be the very word of God—the Bible.

Sadly, not everyone reads their Bibles today—not even Christian leaders—and yet need this solid foundation to know ourselves, know and understand one another, and ultimately to know Christ—His ways, His teachings. If we do not fully know Him, how can we reflect Him in our leadership? Knowing the Bible is to learn to know Him—and this is key to any leadership that is "Christian leadership." For, you see, the Bible convicts our hearts, shows us who we are, and teaches us who we need to be. Reading the Bible matters, but so does the deep study of the Bible. By studying the Bible, we learn, we grow, we transform into the calling of Christ-like leadership.

At times, we know concepts from the world of business, ministry, or organizational life—we take the culture's ways and try to adapt them to our manner of leading. But, you see, this is a false foundation that appears to be strength but is lacking in the depth and solidification of His ways and truths that will keep us encouraged as leaders for the duration of the journey. Dr. Furume unpacks these seemingly simple concepts by delving into scriptural perspectives of ideas, such as communication, vision, team building, trust, success, and even failure. Failure is an interesting concept that we tend to avoid, but this book will show you the great lessons learned here and how to biblically keep moving as a leader and learn from all your moments. When you have hidden God's word in your heart (Psalm 119:11), you will know the path forward and avoid the many pitfalls leaders can find themselves in—you will be well-guided.

Dr. Furume invites you, the reader, into this deep devotion with this book—we are all invited to "more" in our leadership. A solid foundation is laid, a beginning for our understanding of biblical approaches to leadership, and while it may seem you have read this book before, think again—this foundation is laid out to inform the readers in new ways to understand how and why we need the Bible in our leadership. No matter where you are in your leadership journey, this book will bless and encourage you to look well beyond the world's ideas and know the true path to your leadership journey from a biblical perspective.

Kathleen Patterson, PhD

Professor

Director, Doctor of the Strategic Leadership Program

President, Regent Faculty Senate, School of Business and

Leadership, Regent University

Preface

Growing up, I witnessed firsthand how leadership plays a crucial role in everyday life. However, I separated leadership from my belief and convinced myself that being a believer did not require understanding biblical leadership principles. Yet my struggle with the intertwined relationship of leadership and Christian faith started to manifest and intensify when I had to follow other leaders and finally take on leadership roles.

A common misconception I found about leadership is that many relate to it based on a person and miss the revelation that leadership is not a person; instead, it is the vision and the action in a person. A leader is not who you are but what you carry and how you act. God, speaking to Jeremiah, said in Jeremiah 1:5 (New International Version), *"Before I formed you in the womb, I knew you, before you were born, I set you apart; I appointed you as a prophet to the nations."* This verse can be understood as: "I saw the content of your ability before it manifested itself. Henceforth, I gave you the position to match the function."

In essence, my goal is to explain and demonstrate that leadership is a godly concept, and the Bible should be an essential reference when it comes to leadership and being a leader.

Introduction

> *"Teach me your ways, O LORD, that I may live according to your truth! Grant me purity of heart, so that I may honor you."*
> —Psalm 86:11 (New Living Translation)

Before I knew what I know about leadership, I reduced it to a position within a hierarchy. Hence, I considered a leader to be anyone who held a position that placed them above people. It is accurate and not utterly false if one chooses to ignore the true essence hidden in the notion of leadership.

However, when we need to look at leadership through the lens of the value it holds. Leadership is not simply a position but the value, the knowledge, and the impact it produces and bestows. Kouzes and Posner (2004, 1) expressed their surprise and concern about the narrow understanding of leadership found during their research years. They concluded that the prevailing assumption is that leadership is connected to people's behaviors at the top. The belief is that leadership is somewhat only accessible to few people while "the rest are doomed to leadership incompetence of the superstar executives."

This book is for all aspiring and current leaders, especially Christian leaders who are willing to be "salt and light of the world" (Matthew 5:13–16 (NIV)), and reverence God with their work. The constant issues this generation faces have highlighted the necessity to raise, equip, and send out believers with the fear of the Lord, a well-defined vision, and pure motives in key leadership positions. Because "this generation faces problems that defy easy solutions yet face them we must" (Payleitner 2018, 7).

This book is written with the objective of unveiling biblical truths about leadership. The manuscript reviews historical evidence found in the Bible that helped build leadership's theory and position. Leadership is a well-envied position, a transformation journey from being appointed or rising as a leader to encoding the transferable leadership ability. This book approaches leadership from a biblical standpoint, using successful and failed leadership examples within the scriptures that can help shape the conception and knowledge of the reader. There is no new gaffe in life, only new people committing known and old ones. Knowing essential keys that make up leadership, the reasons why some leaders succeeded and some failed might be a cornerstone in the making of an effective Christian leader in today's society.

This book closes with study questions to help readers apply their learned knowledge to real-life scenarios and gain wisdom for their leadership journey.

Part One
Leadership Is

Chapter One

What Is Leadership?

Those who are wise will shine like the brightness of the heavens, and those who lead many to righteousness, like the stars for ever and ever.
—*Daniel 12:3 (NIV)*

According to Northouse (2015, 6), leadership is an extremely attractive and greatly regarded commodity that seems to get everyone's attention yet causes a lot of controversy in its application: "Leadership is a process that involves influence and occurs in a group in order to reach common goals."

As Genesis 1 demonstrates, *the process* aspect of leadership entails that it is a journey with a starting point and an ending point if not handled properly, or an infinite path that multiplies itself in others, while impacting the environment in which it flourishes.

Shakeel, Kruyen, and Van Thiel (2019) debated that leadership should not be approached as a style that one adopts, rather as a process that molds and transforms not just the followers and environment but more so the leader himself. In that journey, the leader discovers himself, his purpose, his abilities, and his inabilities.

As an illustration, we can compare leadership to a selected seed that is planted and is expected to go through the whole germination process in order to grow the plant within its embryonic axis. The seed, then, is said to contain the plant within it, and the plant carries seeds in it. This will spark the debatable question that we will later address in chapter four, "Are Leaders Born or Made?" Regardless, Jennings and Stahl-Wert (2016, 1) believe the germination process is actually a "story about personal growth and how good leaders become great leaders through their willingness to face and be changed by the greatest challenges of their lives."

The influence's feature of leadership is portrayed in Strock's slightly revised definition of leadership. For him, it is "the killer app that can transform all aspects of life and work. Its principles are universal, but its applications diverge depending on the realities at hand and how one can create the greatest values in the circumstances" (2018, 18).

Leadership and influence go hand in hand. Apart from influence, leadership would not exist (Northouse 2015). For a seed to germinate, it needs a fertile ground. We can conclude from it that the fertility or the state of the environment plays a major role in the growth of a seed. This is exactly what leadership is. As a leader, one becomes the fertile ground upon which the seeds in the vision and followers have the ability to produce and reproduce itself.

Influence:
a. "The capacity to have an effect on someone's beliefs or actions.
b. A person or thing with the capacity to affect someone's beliefs or actions.
c. The power arising out of status or wealth" (Waite 2013, 469).

Influence in leadership is, hence, its currency (Scroggins 2017). The result of the transformative impact a person has on people because the effectiveness of leadership is seen in the scope of results it produces. Effective influence happens when "iron sharpens iron" in people (Proverbs 27:17). According to Maxwell (2007, 11), "the true measure of leadership is influence—nothing more, nothing less." Because true leadership cannot be conferred, allotted, or appointed. It comes only from influence, and that cannot be delegated. "It must be earned. The only thing a title can buy is a little time either to increase your level of influence with others or to undermine it" (13). As difficult as reaching the stature of influence may be, many like Sosik and Jung (2018) agree that it remains an effective way for leaders to magnify on their leadership reach.

When it comes to influence, the key agent is not the leader but the people in the group. As influential as a leader can be, if he does not have followers, it serves no purpose. That is why one of the first things God does when He chooses a person is to point them toward the scope of their calling and the audience upon which they are called. In other words, unseal the mystery of the audience they have and need to influence. *"Now I am sending you to the king of Egypt so that you can lead my people out of his country,"* Exodus 3:10 (Good News Translation) said.

Inspiring others does not just strengthen the relationship between the leader and the subordinates by creating an environment of trust and reliability, but it also gives a sense of autonomy of thoughts and accountability in action. When elementary psychological needs are met, they enable people to act and flourish in a given environment.

Leadership is not about collecting followers but raising more leaders, because active followership is rooted in inspired leadership. In other words, a group "is highly unlikely to move forward without effective leadership that inspires the followers to be led" (Jerry 2013, 345–348). It is not just for the leader to solve the problem but also to inspire people to get on board to find a solution to the problem. That is what influence does.

The people characteristic of leadership insinuates an inclusive leadership that partners with people rather than uses people to reach a given goal (Ciulla 2014). When a seed understands that the only way for it to produce anything is to partner with the elements in the ecosystem, it does not struggle to receive the support and nutrients from the soil, the oxygen from the air, and more. In fact, it is believed that a seed will remain dormant or inactive until conditions are met for germination.

It is almost impossible for anyone to effectively witness the full range of their leadership blossom unless it occurs in a group. "Grand dreams do not become significant realities through the actions of a single leader, because leadership is a team effort" (Kouzes and Posner 2004, 87).

For that reason, although the leadership journey might feel lonely, it is not a journey of and to loneliness. It is a building journey that requires the bricks and hands of all to build the tallest and strongest envisioned tower. Nehemiah had the vision to rebuild the walls of Jericho, yet it was the contribution of all that partnered with him that made it possible despite the numerous oppositions. In the words of Maxwell (2007, 298–300), "if it is lonely at the top, you are not doing something right because no one ever got to the top alone and taking people to the top is what good leaders do." Unfortunately, many do not understand the shared meaning birthed out of collaboration with people and miss on the opportunity "to influence people, create a positive result, and change things" (Adams and Anderson 2016, 2).

Leaders are far from being simple superstars at the top. They are called to nurture a transformative environment for their followers to flourish and one day be prepared enough to take upon the leadership baton. Leadership is serving others while transforming people. King Solomon understood that the competitive advantage he had, compared to other kingdoms, would bring results if it serves the cause of the people. "The serving leader is down here unleashing the strengths, talents, and passions of those he or she serves. It works this way for a team of two, a business with a thousand employees, or a community of several million" (Jennings and Stahl-Wert 2016, 23).

As part of working with people, a confident leader should not be afraid to share the stage with his followers because he understands that his role as a leader is not to control power and performance. Instead, it is to distribute it by enabling others to act on behalf of the team to reach the common goal. Hodgson (1985) wrote that more leaders are finding a need to spend their time leading from within rather than from outside their groups. Hence, real leadership speaks for "us," not for "me," and the worth of the common goal should outweigh personal agenda.

The common goal feature of leadership focuses on the joint purpose people have within a group. A team with no purpose is subject to confusion because direction plays a crucial role in leadership. A leader has to be able to point the followers toward the final destination. Hackman and Johnson (2013, 401) advise to "build momentum by successfully completing a series of small steps. Small victories build momentum for greater changes."

A vision never dies; with time, it either grows or reinvents itself. The COVID-19 pandemic took the world by surprise in 2020. If there is anything to learn from it, no one is ever too prepared for what is coming ahead. Hence, plan for growth and expansion, but do not despise planning for a backup strategy to sustain the common goal in case of an emergency that can threaten the group's well-running.

The plan should not just be about saving the leader but also the team and, if possible, the community it serves. After the fall of man in Genesis 3, God unleashed a salvation plan that not only helped sustain but also restored and improved the common goal. Greenleaf (2002) argued that community should not be lost in the process of development because where there is no community, fundamental life values such as trust, respect, and ethical behavior are hard to acquire and uphold. This is where servant-leadership is essential "to show the way, not by mass movements but by each servant-leader demonstrating his unlimited liability for a quite specific community-related group" (39).

As a leader, the individual has to be able to bring the future into the present of the group because a vision is nothing, but a present-day explanation of a futuristic idea of how something ought to be. Henceforth, it is crucial for leaders to be futuristic, revolutionary, and innovative in their vision casting and implementation because the present is the past of the future. The real impact of the common goal should be to go across culture and beyond the geographical barrier; it should have a global context and embrace diversity.

If the common goal is to sustain the ecosystem, then the seed which grew to a plant knows that its purpose is to become the primary food source for the soil in the ecosystem, and the soil understands that it needs to provide the needed support and nutrients to grow the seed to the plant in return.

What is leadership then? More than being about an individual, leadership is the process of discovery and influence manifested within a group that is working toward a common objective.

Chapter Two

Leadership Is God-Ordained

In the beginning God created . . .
—Genesis 1:1 (NIV)

Then God said, "Let us make mankind in our image, in our likeness, so that they may rule over the fish in the sea and the birds in the sky, over the livestock and all the wild animals, and over all the creatures that move along the ground."
—Genesis 1:26 (NIV)

Understanding the relationship between leadership and the divine requires meticulously delving into biblical texts. Biblical scriptures were written in a spiritual context, using several aspects of mankind's life that depicts the interaction between divinity and humanity. For instance, in Jeremiah 29:11, when God was confirming His intention toward the house of Israel. Also, in historical and literary contexts in which the different authors relate the spiritual, social, religious, economic, and political circumstances that existed at a particular time and place in biblical time like in the books of Exodus and the 1 and 2 Kings. Troster (2011) explained that "the Bible is not a book; it is a library. It has many books with often very different ideas about God, humanity, and the world."

The transliteration of the Bible caused some of the wording to be changed, adapted, withdrawn, and added to fit the grammatical context of the language in which it was written. However, it is essential to note that it does not, in any way, change the intended purpose for which it was written. In fact, Duvall and Hays (2012) commented that "the process of getting the Bible in a given language goes from inspiration from a divine author to transmission to human authors (Hebrew, Aramaic, and Greek), then translation and interpretation into the receptor language" (24).

What better way to look into the divine purpose of leadership than starting in the genesis of creation? Genesis 1 begins with the story of God working, innovating, creating, and delegating. Genesis 1:1—"In the beginning God created . . ." (NIV). The root meaning of the word *beginning*—H7225, "resit"—refers to order or rank (especially, first fruit and principal thing), from the same name group as H7218—"ros"—which converts to *chief, chiefest place, captain, forefront,* and *ruler,* (Strong 2007, 1571). It can be implied here that Genesis 1:1 introduced us to not just the leadership of God but leadership by and from God, which, through the first three chapters of the book, establishes divine leadership principles that we commonly see applied in today's society. Principles related to personal development, skills development, relational development—in other words, the full range of leadership development.

The most exciting aspect of His work and leadership is that God did it to better things around Him (Genesis 1:2) and innovatively helped the rest of creation by generating a system of autonomous yet connected ecosystems. God used His creativity and communication ability to speak things into existence and His artistic skill to form things. Every single thing He created, even the least of them, had a purpose that not only benefited itself but systematically and enigmatically benefited the rest of creation. This is indeed what leadership is about: quality connection across all established relationships with the aim of producing something beautiful and uninterrupted (Genesis 1:31, 2:1–3).

The first three chapters of Genesis introduce leaders to the type of relationships they can encounter in their journey: (1) the intrapersonal relationship, which is the relationship with self, and (2) the interpersonal relationship, which refers to the relationship with others. Healthy and godly leadership means being on good terms with yourself, God, and others, because creativity and innovation flows best when your inner self is on good terms. Referring back to Genesis 1:1, the root word for *God* is actually Elohim—H430—the plural for El'oah—H433. This pluralistic reference comes back all through chapters one, two, and three, a way of displaying the agreement and harmony within the Godhead to bring forth creation. Effective leaders do not fight their vision; they come in agreement and alignment with themselves first, then with others to reach the common goal.

The intrapersonal aspect of leadership is seen in Genesis 1:27–30, where we see the first ever recorded interaction between the divine and the human: A firsthand follower recruitment and delegation, which turned into a leadership appointment of humankind over the rest of creation. After the creation of man (Genesis 1:27), God rested from His work, which He qualified as "very good" (Genesis 1:27). Upon resting, He delegated man to watch over His creation, subdue and multiply it—in other words, He delegated man to work (Genesis 1:28–30). See, work is not a chore on mankind; it is a responsibility, a right, and duty for anyone aspiring to lead.

Two of the primary themes of this passage is creation and work. The effectiveness of leadership is in the ability to create and produce a result out of one's work. Leaders work to create and innovate. God spoke to himself and advise himself to create a being that resembled Him so He can take charge of their creation. He also gave that person (man) the ability to multiply his species and expand all over the earth. "Man and woman were given the role of theocratic administrators who would co-rule God's creation on his behalf" (Hindson and Yates 2012, 55).

Witherington (2016) defines work as any obligatory and momentous duty that God requests and "gifts a person to do and which can be assumed to the glory of God and for the edification and aid of human beings, being inspired by the Spirit and presaging the realities of the new creation" (xii). From the definition, two crucial elements help understand work and purpose from a biblical and Christian perspective: God calls man to work and enables him to perform that work.

From God's example in Genesis 1, we learn that leadership's work should lead to creation, innovation, transformation, and appreciation. He took time to transform the chaotic darkness that was around him, and once it produced a satisfying result, He appreciated that. Witherington (2016) clarifies that a doctrinal understanding of work is only acceptable if it enables "transformation of work toward ever-greater correspondence with the coming new creation" (xv).

Genesis teaches that humanity came from God's nature and will. "The decision was an expression of God's character: creative, relational, loving. God created the world to say something about himself, to extend His relational nature to embrace beings who bear His image, and to communicate with them" (Fackler 2006, 1). As He transferred and shared His leadership with man, He also transferred His work ethic to him. When it comes to working, Fackler (2006) explained that human beings are the only creatures with moral responsibility and accountability, unlike any other species. As an appointed ruler of the earth, man is expected to take care of it, multiply it, and preserve it. After all, he has been entrusted with living and seed-bearing creatures—in other words, seed-bearing potential. Only a called person can understand that reality about work and apply the gift received to fulfill the work. Witherington (2016) puts it this way: "Calling and work go together in the kingdom" (13). If you feel called to lead, know that you are called to create, innovate, transform, and delegate.

Genesis is the book of the beginning—not just of creation but of leadership as a science, a position, and theory. Its chapters one and two detail the sequential order of the creation of the physical universe by Elohim (God), as well as the start of the human race. Everything that exists today has its spiritual root in God's creative mind as it is written in Genesis 1:1.

According to Hindson and Yates (2012), "all things owe their existence to His almighty fiat 'word'" (55). Genesis 1:26–30 is part of a more significant descriptive event that happened at the beginning of humanity. It starts in Genesis 1:1 with God, then moves to the separation of light and darkness, to the naming of day and evening, and the creations of luminaries, vegetation, animals, and so forth. On the sixth day, as the verses mention, God created man.

God, as the ultimate leader, introduced himself and His vision. He went on to initiate creation, transformation, and innovation, then dealt with any shades of confusion by bringing light in.

God as the central character is mentioned six times by His Hebrew name "Elohim," and eight times pronouns, such as I, us, He, his, and our, are used to refer to God. There are three occurrences of the verb "to say" and "to create," and two references of the verb "to give," and one mention of the verb "to bless" that emphasize the action taken by God toward the existence of the humankind. This shows the emphasis put on the leader's role. As you rise to that position, do not sit on a seat of comfort; communicate and create more and you will see satisfactory results.

On the other side, the verb "to rule" and "to be" are used to refer to man's purpose in creation. The repetitive texture in Genesis 1:26–30 demonstrates the trajectory upon which man had dominion, and the words "every" and "all" specify the quantity upon which the dominion is extended. The potential to grow the influence of your leadership is hidden in your understanding of "every and all" declared by God in Genesis 1. This will also help you understand and embrace the scope of your talent.

The presence of the conjunction "so" in verse 26 present a cause-and-effect result that occurred during creation that point toward the divine establishment of leadership. Leadership was instilled in mankind's DNA.

The Cause: God made man in His image and likeness.

The Effect: Man can now rule.

This evidence backs up Maxwell's (2018) claim that leadership is a God-ordained ability that allows man to lead and rule, but only within the framework of God's leadership.

There are occurrences of listed items such as "image" and "likeness" in verse 26 to refer to the features of man and "the fish," "the plants," "the birds," "the wild animals," and "all the creatures" in verse 26 to 28 to state man's possession and resources, then "male" and "female" in verse 27 to discuss the kind of mankind that was created; "be fruitful," "increase," "fill," "subdue," and "rule" to describe mankind's purpose and assignment on earth.

Leadership is, hence, the divinely ordained ability to reproduce, rule, subdue, or, even better, make more leaders with divine qualification for effective leadership. The reoccurring verbs used to describe God's action during creation are "make" and "create." Man was made (*Asah*—H6213) and created (*Bara*—H1254); the rest of creation was only created (*Bara*) as DeWitt (2007) explains. The fact that man is the pinnacle of God's creative work is evident from his designation as God's image bearer. In fact, the root meaning of *Bara* (H1254) means to qualify, dispatch, and select. Next to the verb "to rule," it demonstrates the possibility of what man can do based on the expressed desire of God to make humankind in His image and His likeness. In this passage, God spoke first to himself when He said, "Let us," then He spoke to the male and female He created to lay down their purpose.

There are multiple leadership principles to grasp here. The first principle is leadership as his resemblance. We are a creation in the image of God, and we possess God's attributes (likeness) inside of us. We have received all power and authority from God to rule and subdue over the rest of creation. Although there are transferable skills needed, what you need the most as a leader is hidden inside of you in a container called the "image and likenesses" of the one who created, called, and established you.

The second principle is of relationship. From the beginning of humankind's existence to today, He has always been with men, probably because they are the only creature He can relate to as far as appearance and resemblance go. This verse portrays the intimate God, who took time to form a being that had much of

Him in him. One of the biggest mistakes a leader can make is to ignore the power of relationship. For a player, a puzzle can only make sense when each piece is related to the other. Each one of the relationships you have as a leader plays some kind of role to the building or rebuilding of your walls.

The third principle is empowerment that comes out of this passage, as a leader God was not afraid to delegate someone else over His work. Humans have received power and authority from God to have dominion over creation and all living creatures. However, it does not stop there. One of the next assignments is to multiply. You have failed as a leader if you have not multiplied yourself in others. Jesus multiplied himself in twelve disciples and more than fifty other men following him. These men also multiply themselves in thousands of others and so on. Multiplication is a requirement to leadership. Paul said to Timothy, "And the things you have heard me say in the presence of many witnesses entrust to reliable people who will also be qualified to teach others" (2 Timothy 2:2 (NIV)).

The fourth principle is the principle of divine appointment. It is God that appoints, although people can elect. Only those chosen by God make it to the position of leadership; however, it is their observance of divine principles of leadership that will play a role in determining the kind of impact they make. As a believer, do not feel restrained to involve God in your journey; seek Him in your ways, turn to Him for wisdom and counsel, and talk to Him if you need a friend.

Chapter Three

Leadership Is a Mind-Set

*In your relationships with one another,
have the same mindset as Christ Jesus.*
—Philippians 2:5 (NIV)

The divine leadership journey of mankind is not only portrayed in Genesis. The rest of the Bible, on numerous occasions, affirms and confirms that man looks like God and therefore can reproduce and dominate as God has ordained it. All throughout the Bible, evidence of the divine leadership appointment of mankind was often subject to confusion, conflict, and more.

The psalmist in the book of Psalm 8:3–8 asks an essential question as to why God decided to glorify man that way by giving him such an important position. The gospel of Matthew 5:8 addresses the source of man's perfection, which is God and in God. In the New Testament, Jesus Christ is "the image of the invisible God, the firstborn over all creation" (Colossians 1:15 (NIV)); He is also "the radiance of His glory and the exact representation of His nature, and upholds all things by the word of His power when He had made purification of sins, He sat down at the right hand of the Majesty on high" (Hebrews 1:3 (NIV)).

The intentional relationship of God toward men is seen all over the Bible as God often initiated the encounter with humankind despite all the shortcomings of men. Remember, "it is not the words that make a response reflect the attitude, it is always the heart behind the words" (Gutierrez 2012, 83). After the fall of man described in Genesis 3:1–24, and the separation that occurred between men and Him, God started working on a plan of redemption that was fulfilled on the cross by Jesus Christ (Luke

23:26–43). Jesus became, therefore, the expression of God's love for men (Romans 5:8). We learn from this that leadership is not just about the ruling over things, it is also in the mind-set reflecting the love and servant's heart leaders have for their followers sometime at their most undesirable moment.

Understanding that men may elect a leader, but it is God who calls the person and equips the mind to grasp the depth and responsibility—that is leadership. Indeed, it is God who establishes all authority and equips for the function (Daniel 2:21; John 19:11; and Romans 13:1). Hence, we see occurrences in the Bible where God had to first transform the mind-set of his elects, bring it to a place of acceptance, before working through them. Steward, Mann, and Jakes (2020) commented that a God-ordained leadership demands taking a leap of faith while looking beyond what is safe for the human mind, because the reality we have experienced often prohibits our mind to grasp the potential God sees in us.

According to Anderson and Adams (2016, 31), leadership consciousness begins in the mind, because "it is the inside game of leadership. It is the leader's inner operating system." What pushes the leader, how they see themselves, what is imperative to them, and what they consider. The more developed the inner game, the more efficient a leader's outer game, because the inner game runs the outer game.

Victory begins in the mind. You cannot conquer the battle your mind has not won. You cannot win the victory your mind does not see. God knew that one of the first steps to empowering a person called is to address their mind-set so it can influence their behaviors (Romans 12:2). According to Strock (2018), having a growth mind-set that leaves room for one to commit to learning, instead of stubbornly maintaining past knowledge, is what will set and make one effective as leaders.

Judges 6, 7, 8, and 9 are prime examples that portray how leadership is more effective when it flows from the mind-set. Gideon, the least in his father's house, from the poorest family, was chosen by God; however, his mind-set was not yet wired for the vision and victory God entrusted him. His mind-set concerning leadership was renewed after he faced seven leadership realities:

1. The eureka moment (Judges 6:11–13)
2. The doubt moment (Judges 6:13, 15)
3. The discovery moment (Judges 6:14, 17)
4. The sacrifice moment (Judges 6:19–26)
5. The recruitment moment (Judges 6:27–30; 7:1–8)
6. The challenge moment (Judges 7:9)
7. The mission moment (Judges 7:16–25)
8. The victory moment (Judges 6:7–8)

The eureka moment (Judges 6:11–13): The young Gideon with low self-esteem had a transforming encounter that exposed him to the call in his life. However, as previously mentioned, his mind did not comprehend such a high calling upon his life when the reality around him called for something different. How can one be called to something great when the reality at end demonstrates the contrary?

One way is to understand and accept that "when God raises a leader, He gives him the capacity to make things happen" (Engstrom and Mooneyham 1976, 19). Hence, authority is not the prerequisite for leadership. You do not have to wait to be somebody or hold a title for you to feel adequate to lead. Leadership demands "a clear understanding of one's identity as a leader, apart from any titles," Scroggins (2017, 35) said.

Gideon had already given up on much of his calling because of what his people were going through with their oppressors and the unfulfilled promises announced to them. A great lesson to learn here concerning the eureka moment in leadership is that, often, a leader's niche is found in what he considers a struggle or a challenge. Moses struggled with the way the Egyptians were treating the people of Israel. Little did he know that the area of his frustration was the place of his calling; he was called to free them from the hands of Pharaoh (Exodus 3:10). Man sinned and was separated from God; that struggle that came with the consequences of disobedience became the reason why He had to come to the rescue of humanity (Romans 5:10).

The doubt moment (Judges 6:13, 15): Just like with anything great that can happen, sometimes it may sound or look too good to be true. In fact, Psalm 126:1 says, "When the Lord restored the fortunes of Zion, we were like those who dreamed" (English Standard Version). It is true that doubt sometimes carries a negative connotation with it, but it is also essential to know that in the process of comprehending one's leadership calling, doubt will sometimes manifest not because God, who called us, cannot trust us, use us, or does not know us, but more because we have to accept ourselves and the grace in our lives from God's perspective.

Most fears are a natural outgrowth of change (Bellman 2002, 88). Hence, the doubt moment manifests itself in many through the fear to take risk. For Steward, Mann, and Jakes (2020), the greatest risk in any venture is not the investment of good, time, or what one does but the investment of who the person is. For Gideon, he was just the least of the least that is often oppressed by the Midianites; but for God, he was more than that. He was strong, he had a calling and a purpose, he was mandated, and he was a great warrior. In the midst of doubt, it is always best to rely on and refer to God. Do not be wise in your own eye, and do not rely on your own understanding. Be humble enough to submit all your ways to him so he can make your paths straight, as Proverbs 3:5–8 suggests.

The discovery moment (Judges 6:14, 17): So many people presume already knowing who they are and what they are supposed to do but as for a good majority of biblical leaders, they learned about the difference between their identity and their calling all throughout their journey. Moses's identity was tied to Egypt, yet his calling made him an enemy to Egypt (Exodus 2 and 3). One of the main reasons being that leadership is not just about influencing others but also being influenced by others. Leadership is not just about what you speak but more about the application of what you speak. It is also a journey of discovery, self-awareness, appreciation, and acceptance of the leader to the leader.

According to Reagin (2018), the discovery moment is the foundation of a lifetime of leading well. "Knowing yourself unchains your leadership potential. You can't lead genuinely without knowing your true self. To lead authentically, you first have to prune the lies and nurture the truths" (51–52). You are not your mission; rather, your identity supports your mission and unveils more of your responsibilities.

Esther almost forsook her Hebrew identity for the comfort of her mission's field. Forgetting, or perhaps ignoring, the fact that what God can do through us includes us, but does not depend on us (Stearns 2021). Thanks be to Mordecai who reminded her that forsaking her identity for such reason can lead to her own end.

"He sent back this answer: 'Do not think that because you are in the king's house you alone of all the Jews will escape. For if you remain silent at this time, relief and deliverance for the Jews will arise from another place, but you and your father's family will perish. And who knows but that you have come to your royal position for such a time as this?'" (Esther 4:13–14 (NIV)).

As a called leader, you have to accept the fact that social rank, education, association, and so forth are assets to leadership, but they are not the ultimate for success in leadership. Leadership begins in the mind, grows with the mind, and is the expression of our preconceived mind-set. The discovery moment in leadership is not something we rehearse; rather, it is an attitude we learn to foster. "Developing a habit of self-discovery means designing intentional rhythms whereby one observes who he is, listens to his life, and strives to define himself apart from his professional assignments. Unless one is rooted in his identity, he can never become a change maker," Lomenick and Burnett (2015, 5) wrote.

As a rising leader, explore the ability within you and give yourself the chance to learn, even if it means failing once or twice. In your discovery season, do not sit on what did not work for you or what could have worked; pull the lesson out of that expression, learn from it, and evolve.

Acceptance during the discovery moment happens when one accepts to tolerate their imperfection and shake off the preconceived idea of perfection before leading, because no one is perfect, and all have flaws that make us the weakest and least (Romans 3:23; Judges 6:15) because our imperfection is not our identity. According to Greenleaf (2002), it is part of the paradox of human nature that the typical imperfect person is capable of great commitment and heroism if wisely led, while the otherwise able people are ineligible to lead by their pride, which cause them to fall (Proverbs 16:18; 3:34; James 4:10; 1 Peter 5:5).

The sacrifice moment (Judges 6:19–26): Nothing great in this world is ever served in a plate of gold. It takes sacrifice and dedication to go for what we believe in. That is why it is important to already hold a sacrificial mind-set and accept the fact that leadership success demands sacrifice and service.

According to Denning (2007, 76), leadership sacrifice should not just be "a mental commitment but a commitment of mind, body, and soul to making things happen and sharpen the focus on the goal." Paul in Romans 12:1 (NIV) urged the believers to offer their bodies or their faculties (Weymouth 2017) as living sacrifice. In other words, to wholeheartedly surrender all of themselves to God. Boa, Buzzell, and Perkins (2007) believe that effective leadership flows from a consecration to the right things. As followers of Christ, the single most important commitment of our lives is to God. Any true (and eternal) success we experience as leaders will flow from that devotion.

As leaders we have to commit our fear, our exploits, and all there is under the authority of the one who has called and equipped us so that as we are pursuing the calling and fulfilling the vision, the one we are committed to is also working in us to the perfection of that commitment. "A surrendered leader has nothing left to lose because they have already put everything in God's hands," Stearns (2021) wrote.

The eureka, doubt, and discovery moment birth passion in leadership, which in turn births commitment to the vision. It is that commitment that causes leaders to be willing to pay the price required to see the vision come to pass. According to Kouzes and Posner (2006, 18), "nothing great is ever accomplished without making sacrifices"; greatness comes with a cost. By sacrificing, a leader proves that he is not in it for selfish interest because sacrifice sends the message, loud and clear, that the heart of the leader is wired on the common goal not individual ambition.

Once Gideon started wrapping his mind around his calling, he asked the angel to wait for him as he was preparing his sacrificial offering. A way of saying that, if it was for me, I'll not just be okay with seeing the unjust social condition of my family improved but I choose today to sacrifice for the greater calling you are calling me to. The quality of the result one can produce is also dependent on the sacrifice and work they put into that. Just as it seemed for Gideon, sacrifice may feel like the end of us, but if we understand that we are "not going to die" from the work and dedication we put into the development of our full-range leadership, maybe it will give us more peace to endure the effort it takes.

The recruitment moment (Judges 6:27–30; 7:1–8): As it has been mentioned on numerous occasions, leadership is not about the leader and whatever he may benefit from it. The true result of effective leadership is seen in the quality of followers it produces. It is common to hear people say, "self-made man." However, it may shock many to know today that there is no such thing as a self-made man because, even if they do not appear in the spotlight, there are plenty of hands that worked in secret to help sculpt the man that has succeeded in public. Chapter 6 and 7 of Judges may only mention Gideon's name but there are three hundred more unnamed heroes that walked with him in this leadership journey.

Leadership success demands, as Sanborn (2017) advises, engaging others and building mutually beneficial relationships that will leverage your work while empowering them. Proverbs

11:25 (NIV) says it best: "A generous person will prosper; whoever refreshes others will be refreshed." Those that fail to do it and choose to do everything by themselves without involving others limit their productivity and may be more prone to burn out, or worse, a failure (Steward, Mann, and Jakes 2020).

One of the easiest ways to engage people is by building a team and investing in them. The sooner one wraps his mind around the responsibility, the right and duty of building a team, the quicker they can invest in the ins and outs of what it takes to have a solid team. We will address the ins and outs of building a team in chapter seven of this book. A solid team will help support the vision and the visionary so that the given mandate can be achieved. The right team keeps your hands lifted as you are trying to accomplish the 'almost impossible task of leadership (Exodus 17:12–14).

Later, in chapter seven of the book of Judges, God intervenes in the team-building process in Gideon's leadership. The important lesson to learn here is that God is as more invested in transforming leaders' mind-sets when it comes to team building than in empowering the leader. His strategy with Gideon was to make him realize that quantity will never surpass quality. It is best to have a small team made of quality participants than having the largest team with inadequate team members or little to no time to invest in them. As Judges 7:1–3 demonstrate, sometimes too many is not good; three hundred dedicated members is way better than tens of thousands of undecided and uncommitted people.

The challenge moment (Judges 7:9): Challenges are part of the leadership journey. Every single aspect of leadership is a challenge in itself that requires willpower to tackle them. For that reason, it is important to know that leadership is not for the faint of heart because it challenges all aspects of a leader's existence. According to Kouzes and Posner (2006), challenges in leadership can be doorways to innovation and progressive change. Hence, as you embark in the leadership journey, prepare your mind to the possibility of encountering challenges that may seem frightening at first but not necessarily impossible when you take upon them.

Reagin (2018, 113–114) equates the challenge moment to the call to sweat and said that "hard work will always be a requirement of life-giving leadership because success and leadership require massive amounts of sweat and hustle." Nevertheless, remember that proper planning, a good team, and strategy are all part of the leadership strategy that will help you overcome anything that comes your way. Do not just act—act with tact even while you are afraid of the challenges before you. What you may not understand now is that the tests before you are afraid of you.

Gideon was frightened by the idea of going after the Midianites, the Amalekites, and all the other eastern peoples. The latter ones were talking among themselves about what was about to happen to them because of Gideon (Judges 7:7–17). God spoke to Gideon about the challenge before him and reassured him of his participation in the process. The confidence to have as Christian leaders is to know that no matter the weight of the challenges you may face in your leadership journey, God sent you and is with you in this journey (Jeremiah 2021).

According to Stearns (2021, 225), most challenges are not black and white in description; they hide themselves in the shades of gray and it is "the leader's job to find clarity in the midst of the grayness." That was exactly what happened to Gideon, he needed to have clarity not only about the strategy in building the right team but also the strategy to win the battle and overcome the challenge.

What followers need in time of challenges is a confident leader that will show them the way and encourage them to act with tact. Being that type of life-giving leader not only empowers and inspires your followers but it encourages and changes you. For a mighty warrior with no tangible victories is just a title carrier and it is just a matter of time before you get questioned. Your victories are what will sustain your title; do not hold back, prepare your mind to embrace challenges.

The mission moment (Judges 7:16–25): The "act with tact" mentioned earlier is what will encompass the mission. More than having a vision of where you want to go, a good leader needs to strategize on the mission to know how he will proceed with the goal. According to Hultman and Gellermann (2002), clarifying the mission will help the leader create a motivational system mapping that will cause him to move toward growth.

As your leadership mind-set is being transformed, remember that mission is part of the mind-set of the leader. A mission-minded leader finds his sense of meaning and purpose from within because his drive for the mission is the reflection of his made-up mind (Kouzes and Posner 2004).

As it unfolds, a mission brings clarity to the vision which, at first, may seem impossible or unrealistic. After accepting his calling, Gideon spent time strategizing on the mission, whether it was through asking questions to the angel or recruiting soldiers and so forth, he made sure that the knowledge acquired through his mind-set-transformation season was bestowed on his followers. He encouraged his followers to do as he was doing.

Gideon's strategy was to divide the three hundred men into three companies. He gave them trumpets and empty jars with torches inside, then commanded them to observe and imitate him. None went out of alignment to pursue their own agenda and "while each man held his position around the camp, all the Midianites ran, crying out as they fled" (Judges 7:21).

Gideon's mission became an opportunity for him to delegate responsibility to his teammates, "splitting their responsibilities in accord with their abilities." This was the only way to defeat their enemies because "it was a team effort or rather, the combined effort of multiple teams," MacArthur (2010) wrote.

The above verse portrays the beauty of owning the mission and letting it impact one another's mind-set. When you are mission-minded, personal agenda and self-sabotage become the least in your priorities as they might get you distracted. Your focus is to hold your position, empower your team, and use what has been made available to you to succeed in your mission and honor God in the process.

The victory moment (Judges 6:7–8): Victory begins in the mind-set. No one who had a loser's mind-set ever won anything. A victor's mind-set fuels ambition and ambition prompts achievement in a leader. Just as it was with creation in Genesis 1, a leader has to speak his victory into existence and convince his mind that he is fit for victory, then pursue that victory. Because of his victorious mind-set, David, the non-military shepherd, won against Goliath, the giant and skillful military man of the Philistine army—a man with a track record of undefeated battles (1 Samuel 17:41–52). David's determination was to defeat the man who tried to dishonor God and shame His people. It is important to note that ambition is the yearning to produce outstanding results. It is "the personal energy to pursue worthy results" (Adams and Anderson 2016, 190).

According to Lomenick and Burnett (2015, 64), although ambition is concealed deep within a person, it still needs to be unearthed because "developing a healthy habit of ambition is one of the most important tasks of every leader" who wants to achieve results. This will help create the momentum in the team because they will know through the leader's confidence and ambitious mind-set that whatever effort they are putting into the vision and the mission is for a victorious outcome.

Working with people that also hold a victorious mind-set makes the work process much more enjoyable than dealing with pessimists who cannot and do not want to see any eventuality of victory or positive outcome. This type of pessimist in a community is also known as "the Nathanaels." These are the people who cannot fathom anything good coming out of Nazareth (John 1:46).

God challenged Gideon's mind-set to allow him to accept and cherish the victory available to him (Judges 6:12–16), then set a high-performance expectation and challenged Gideon to meet them (Judges 6:14). He went on with putting on the side anyone whose mind-set was not yet wired for victory (Judges 7:2–8).

There are numerous possible applications of these leadership-mind-set realities that can help cultivate a victorious mind-set. Here are a few suggested ones:

When struggling with low self-esteem, identity crisis, and things of such, leaders should remember that God knew and appointed them (Jeremiah 1:5). Every feature in them, whether it is external or internal, resembles God's characteristics (Genesis 1:26). Therefore, according to Psalm 139:14, they are wonderfully and fearfully made in His image and likeness and victory is available to them to pursue. DeWitt (2007) points out that man was created by God specially and separately from all the other creatures, the image of God represents His external appearance, and His likeness describes his character. Whenever you feel as if you amount to nothing and there is no purpose for you on earth, just remember that from the beginning, God created you for a purpose and that is to take care of His creation. You are "God's representative clothed with authority and rule as visible head and monarch of the world" (Fausset, Brown, and Jamieson 1961). The highest approval and opinion you should seek is that of God because the only person He consulted to create you was himself (Elohim). Do not live to please men; instead, live for God (Galatian 1:10)

Chapter Four

Are Leaders Born or Made?

*Behold, I made him a witness to the peoples,
a leader and commander for the peoples.*
—Isaiah 55:4 (ESV)

*And Jesus grew in wisdom and stature,
and in favor with God and man.*
—Luke 2:52 (NIV)

The question of what comes first was announced in the introduction of this book with the illustration of the seed and the plant, and it is important to look into it and sort of shade light on this debatable rhetorical subject: are leaders born or made? Both assertions seem to be correct to the extent that it takes a seed to have a tree and a tree to produce seed. Leaders are made by a leader and leaders make leaders.

Let's stay on these two hypotheses to find a common ground of agreement about this topic. If leaders are born, then would there be a necessity to train them for that role so they can acquire the appropriate skills and knowledge needed to be effective? If leaders are made, can innate traits such as charisma and stature be taught to them?

We should agree to disagree that there are some traits in leadership that are not transferable and make people more suitable to leadership. The person has to have it within them. In the instance of Simon Peter, as a follower, he had something about him that always set him apart from the rest of the disciples. It was almost natural to him every time it was exhibited. He was among the first to be chosen as disciples with the promises to be made into a "fisher of men," interpreted as a recruiter of men and a leader among men (Matthew 4:18–19). He asked and answered the hardest questions (Matthew 19:27; John 13:36; Mark 8:14–21; etc.). Peter stepped out in actions when others backed off (Matthew 14:22–33; John 18:10) and acted as leader in the absence of Jesus. Hence, when the time came to appoint a leader, Jesus picked Simon Peter, the disciple that emerged as a leader through the traits and skills he portrayed (Matthew 16:15–19).

Northouse (2016, 8) believes certain individuals have special natural or genetic features and abilities that make them leaders even before being appointed as one, and these are the advantages that differentiate them from non-leaders. He came to the conclusion that "some are leaders because of their formal position in an organization, whereas others are leaders because of the way other group members respond to them."

As shown with Simon Peter, a natural leader can easily be spotted among many. They tend to stand out and even involuntarily, they exude those traits and attract followers to them. They are visionary in their way of approaching matters, they seek to empower and influence people, they are passionate about what they believe in, they are charismatic and know how to communicate.

Even at the young age of twelve, Jesus was already emanating charisma to the point where his knowledge and posture astounded the wise and educated men in Jerusalem (Luke 2:46–52 (NIV)). So was the "boy" Samuel who was ministering before the Lord in 1 Samuel 2:12–26. His remarkable attributes, growth, and seriousness in the presence of the Lord in his work's place, set him aside and caused him to be considered for a leadership position reserved for a certain family group.

On the other hand, made leaders learn, with time, the proper tactics and skills to be successful as leaders. Both born and made leaders can succeed in their role if they remain in the constant posture of learning and never feel satisfied with their current states because there is more to leadership than what one might know at the level they are.

According to Andronovien (2013), leadership is a virtuous

practice and one of the aspects of practice is the historical and contextual foundation which shapes the participants' behaviors toward certain goals while demanding a substantial degree of expertise gained from other participants, past and present, for achieving the given goals. Practice implies growth and expertise and "similarly to habits, practices are an inseparable part of one's personal life. They are the 'stuff' without which any talk of individual personality is essentially meaningless" (120).

Joseph is a practical example of the virtuous practice of leadership (Genesis 37, 39, and 41). He was a born leader that lacked leadership experience, tact, and people skills. From a younger age, he had an idea of where life was taking him. However, his life, as well as the life of many born leaders, is proof that being a born leader is not enough; proper training and experience is needed to be able to be effective in the role of a leader.

See here, whether one is a born leader or an appointed leader, it is essential to humbly stay teachable and open to inputs; that is how one's character and knowledge is sharpened. Luke 2 says that Jesus listened and asked questions, and 1 Samuel 2 and 3 say of Samuel that he was trained by God himself under the leadership of Eli. This makes leadership not merely a position to hold but an effective "tool for spiritual men" (Engstrom and Mooneyham 1976, 25). We will touch more on the topic of mentorship in chapter eleven.

Joseph's first recounted leadership attempt was with his family members and even there he seemed to have failed because of his character. Most of his interactions with others were about how great he was called to be, how his family will bow before his greatness, and how unfitted everybody else was. Joseph did not understand that humility is one of the greatest character skills any leader can have and should portray. As Jesus would later say, "The greatest among you shall be a servant," Matthew 23:11 (NIV) wrote.

Throughout his life experience, we witness transformation in Joseph as he goes past "the making" process of the full range of his leadership development. Every privilege accessible to him was taken away as he was sold as a slave. He learned servant leadership, the virtue of patience, forgiveness, self-control, and more the hard way, some would say. A season that probably molded him to become the best version of himself and to acquire more leadership experiences.

Anderson (2008) called that type of experience virtuous leadership, "a training manual for the virtues needed to lead authentically" (62). Basing himself on the work of Alexander Harvard, he concluded that leadership theory is shaped by four cardinal virtues—prudence, courage, self- control, and justice. Henceforth, effective leadership is primarily a function of character because character is what builds a leader.

As previously explained, even in groups with no known leaders, there is always one individual who stands out from others because of his leadership traits. However, beyond holding a specific position and being charismatic, effective leaders, whether born or nurtured, need to value certain virtues that make them more prone to the leadership task. We will discuss more on the topic of ethics in chapter nine.

As a leader, Jesus made sure his disciples understood the virtues needed for them to be effective leaders in the world. As mentioned earlier, Simon Peter, among the twelve disciples chosen by Jesus, in the Gospel of Mark 1:16–22 and Luke 6:12–16, portrayed in his discipleship journey the four cardinal virtues of Alexander Harvard. Although he was not the lead disciple at that time, his character traits made him a contender for such a role. On top of Peter's characters was added the training he received through his life which was sealed by the special three years training at the feet of Jesus.

Individuals like Joseph and Peter are very engaging when it comes to the team and the vision. Though their maturity is not yet fully developed, they show attributes and interest that point toward a more natural leadership ability in them. More than being theoretical learners, they are practical learners and want hands-on experience from the leader.

For instance, when the disciples faced the contrary wind and Jesus walked on the waters in Matthew 14:22–33, only Peter, among all the disciples, had the gut and was brave enough to challenge himself and trust that no challenge is ever greater than the mind-set in a person. We also see here that the second he started doubting in his mind, he began sinking, and his leader, Jesus, had to come to his rescue. Born leaders are not afraid to try around their leaders because they know that if their leaders can do it then they can also coach them on how to become a better version of themselves and evolve in their leadership journey.

Contrary to Peter and Joseph, Queen Esther had to be pushed out of her comfort zone, taught some leadership characteristics, until she came to the realization that leadership capability was in her. Not much is known concerning Esther's journey prior to the palace; however, we learn from the book of Esther that she was adopted by her uncle Mordecai who became a mentor and coach to her. The book of Esther becomes, then, not just the salvation and redemptive story of the Jews but the leadership journey of a girl who had to discover herself and understand the power and authority dormant within her. She was made a leader and had to go through a journey of discovery of the full range of her leadership development. The story ends with Esther being confirmed at her position and the mission, for which she was appointed queen, fulfilled.

When it comes to the question if leaders are born or trained, Northouse (2016) emphasized that a line of difference should be drawn between leadership as a trait and leadership as a practice. He reported that the trait standpoint indicates that certain people have particular innate or inborn characteristics or potentials that make them leaders. In other words, only a naturally selected group of people can become leaders. The process or practice viewpoint, on the other hand, suggests that "leadership is a phenomenon that resides in the context of the interactions between leaders and followers and makes leadership available to everyone" (8).

Coach Mordecai had to remind Esther that leadership is not an escape ticket that only protects the leader at the expense of the followers. When followers are negatively affected, a leader has failed at his leadership (Esther 4:13). As believers, we all, in one way or another, are called for such a time as this; we either accept it and enter our leadership journey, or we reject it and face whatever consequences that may follow.

We all probably hoped that, by the end of this chapter, we would come to a conclusion that will give advantage to one hypothesis against the other. However, let's agree that whether born or made, we all are given divine gifts (Romans 12:6) which vary from a person to a person to be used for the bettering of the world around us and the advancement of the Kingdom of God.

Part Two
How Some Leaders Succeeded

Introduction

But among you it will be different. Those who are the greatest among you should take the lowest rank, and the leader should be like a servant.
—*Luke 22–26 (NLT)*

Contrary to general beliefs, leadership success is not measured by popularity; instead, by the quality of its results and the lasting impact of the leader on the followers. This implies that to succeed, leaders have to think through certain things. They include their vision and mission to create a common goal with their audience, master their communication skills to know how to connect, and be prepared to build trust and a team by investing in relationships. The following chapters will go in depth on the subjects of vision, communication, team building, and trust.

Chapter Five

Invest in the Vision and Mission

The word of the Lord came to me, saying, "Jeremiah, what do you see?"
And I said, "I see the branch of an almond tree."
—*Jeremiah 1:11 (NIV)*

See, I am doing a new thing! Now it springs up; do you not perceive it?
I am making a way in the wilderness and streams in the wasteland.
—*Isaiah 43:19 (NIV)*

What would leadership be if the leader was unable to see and perceive a future? Let it be established once and for all here: No! Success begins with the vision and the mission one has. Regardless of how charismatic one is, without a vision, leadership serves no purpose. You cannot lead people where your mind has yet arrived, because it is the vision that "guides day-to-day decisions," Bellman (2002, 144) wrote. Investing in your vision and mission is henceforth taking what you see and making it the goal of what you do.

Rolling back to Genesis, God is seen expressing his desire for and to humanity, he sees the chaos in which it existed and envisioned what could be. According to Sosik and Jung (2018), leadership is offering an exciting image of what is essential to consider by linking the past and the present to the future. The present condition of humanity was dark and chaotic, yet God saw the potential of light and the good in it (Genesis 1:31). He articulated a compelling vision to humanity as he spoke things to existence and what was not, came to be.

In the course of the manifestation of his leadership on earth, we see how things were altered and corrupted by people's vain and wicked ambitions. Yet God did not lose sight of his vision to have a creation that exists in harmony with itself and His divinity. One major lesson we learn here from God is that leadership is not a straight-line journey to the envisioned reality. It can be seen as a puzzle journey that forbids one from losing sight of the vision, regardless of the number of broken pieces that need to be assembled or how blurry the destination looks from our present position.

The initial vision of God was to bring light to a chaotic void and formless face of the deep, (Genesis 1:1–2). Then, He created a being with leadership ability that can continue sustaining the work of creation (Genesis 1:26–30). However, when humankind projected leadership outside of God's will (Genesis 3), it caused humanity to enter one of its toughest and darkest eras, where wickedness, arrogance, self-centeredness, and heartlessness rose to challenge God's ultimate leadership and the harmony He intended. *"And God saw that wickedness of man was great in the earth, and that every imagination of the thoughts of his was only evil continually"* (Genesis 6:5 (King James Version)).

According to Maxwell (2018, 1), "Genesis 6 tells us that humankind became so wicked and self-serving that God determined to start over." Still, they failed to follow God and resumed with their wicked ways.

Other than Adam, God is seen sharing His vision for humankind with Noah, who is described as a man who found grace in the eyes of the Lord, a just man and perfect in his generations, and a man who walked with God (Genesis 6:8–9 (KJV)). He confirms Noah's leadership and establishes a covenant with him after the flood and conferred upon him the same mission He gave to Adam. As a leader, Noah was expected to be fruitful, multiply, replenish the earth, subdue, and have dominion over all living creatures (Genesis 9 (KJV)).

Over time, leadership may change in a group, but the vision

remains the same all throughout the mission. The more the team moves in the mission, the closer the team gets to the vision. Maintaining the same mind-set, concerning the vision, allows for succession to be smooth and effective.

Having a vision about how things ought to be is one step; turning it into a mission is another. A vision can become a mission when the leader grasps it, owns it, and shares it. Your effectiveness as a leader starts with the end in mind and should be structured around priorities because your vision offers an overall viewpoint that guides the actions of the team, while your mission describes the team and how it aligns to achieve the vision, Hackman and Johnson (2013, 114) believes.

In the grasping portion, any proclaimed leader should be able to answer the question, "What do you see?" You cannot engage in "what should I do?" if you are unable to answer the initial question pertaining to your sight, what do you see? It is true, as Boa, Buzzell, and Perkins (2007) say, that good leaders see in the vague image the possibility that others do not see. This ability allows them to not be found in the "what now?" or "what shall I do?"

The extent to which you see will determine the length, depth, height, and breadth of your mission and expectation. Keep in mind that a vision is the ability to seek in the present the future you have foreseen. When you see the chaos around you, what do you see as a solution (Genesis 1)? When, like Elisha, an army with horses and chariots surrounds the city and prepares to attack you, what do you do (2 Kings 6:15–16)? When, like Jesus, you are asked about where you are going, how do you reply (John 13:36–38)?

What you see will influence your end reaction and result and allow you to possibly rise above the fear of adversity and uncertainty. Your mind should live where your fear has never been, and that is a brighter and good future.

As a leader, you cannot appreciate and qualify something of good unless you have seen beauty, purpose, and potential through its muddled state. Every answer coming from the "what do you see?" creates the mind-set for the mission because the leader now owns that mandate. Hence, the vision is now the assignment, and the mission is the road or steps to its completion.

We learn from most divinely appointed leaders, especially Jeremiah and Ezekiel the importance of owning a vision. As previously noted, leadership is a mind-set, and you cannot see what your mind-set does not perceive. Your vision empowers your mind-set, and your mind-set has the ability to elevate and transform your way of thinking and doing. God was trying to communicate a vision to Abraham but the circumstances around him did not break the barrier in his mind-set (Genesis 15:1–6; 17:17). God had to take him out of his place of comfort and rest so he can see the bigger picture of the promise He wanted him to grasp: *"And the LORD took him outside and said, 'Now look to the heavens and count the stars, if you are able.' Then He told him, 'So shall your offspring be.' Abram believed the LORD, and it was credited to him as righteousness"* (Genesis 15:5–6 (KJV)).

As a leader or aspiring leader, do not be afraid of the magnitude of the vision you have been entrusted with. As God spoke to Abraham and commanded him to look at the stars, you have to do the same and look at the stars and imagine all the possibilities that can spring out of the vision you have. This is how you will be able to answer the question "what do you see?" Unfortunately, Abraham's vision was limited to one son he could see, "Ishmael," an altered and man-made version of his God-given vision, (Genesis 16; Genesis 17 (KJV)). However, God had a much better and greater vision for him; instead of one son, God had nations and kings in mind. In other words, the outcome of God's vision for Abraham was leadership, posterity, influence, territories, and authority.

God's vision for Abraham was not geographically limited; He wanted to take it global and give him access to spheres of society he could have never imagined. As a visionary, you succeed when your vision is not limited and can serve the needs of more than just those you could see with your eyes. The beginning of Esau's leadership was a failure because he struggled to understand the vision behind the position he held and could not see all the possibilities hidden in it; hence, for a bowl of soup, he sold his legal right (Genesis 25:29–34).

The same way Abraham was unable to count the stars, do not quantify your vision; explore all the possibilities within it. Learn to adapt your plans while holding persistently to the vision, (Maxwell 2018). Dream big and believe in it.

Chapter Six

Invest in Effective Communication

> *An unreliable messenger stumbles into trouble,*
> *but a reliable messenger brings healing.*
> —*Proverbs 13:17 (NLT)*

> *My dear brothers and sisters, take note of this: Everyone should be*
> *quick to listen, slow to speak and slow to become angry.*
> —*James 1:19 (NIV)*

What is beautiful about leadership is that it's a venue that promotes communication—healthy communication at best. You must know that there is no leadership without communication. And, according to the Bible, proper communication requires careful examination of thoughts before expressing it (Proverbs 15:28). It is our ability to communicate that makes or breaks us as leaders. Maxwell (2018) believes individuals commit to a vision when the leader effectively communicates its benefits.

When Jesus began his ministry, he demonstrated such a high level of communication skills to the point where everyone that had an encounter with him was never left the same. He had such confidence and persuasiveness in his speech that his followers grew by the moment (Luke 8:4), and his antagonists were left perplexed, saying among themselves and the people that sent them, "We have never heard anyone speak like this!" (John 7:46 (NLT)).

Communication is "a complex process through which we express, interpret, and coordinate messages with others" (Verderber and Sellnow 2017, 5), to create a shared meaning, to meet social goals, to manage personal identity, and to carry out relationships. It is either verbal or non-verbal, hence the choice to not communicate at all is communication to all. If not a carrier of its own message, nonverbal communication tends to reinforce the verbal communication. Followers watch leaders more than they listen to them because, more than just the words spoken, the actions play a significant role in showing the way and setting the culture of what one believes or how things are supposed to be. Leaders then can control the outcome of their interaction if they learn to take charge of their way of communicating their vision.

The sooner a leader realizes that the capacity to communicate is a multifaceted art, the faster they can invest in improving their communication skills. Apostle Paul, on countless occasions, urged believers to not just talk their walk but also walk their talk, because leadership is not resumed in motivational speeches, leaders should become a message, preferably a positive and impactful one.

As a human being, a believer, and a leader, it is imperative that we understand the two most important communications we have are vertical with God and horizontal with humans. Why should we have a vertical communication with God, many may wonder? The truth is that meaning flows from the constant communication we have with our maker. Although it may not be advertised or admitted, many of the leaders out there are searching for meaning in whatever experience they can have or conviction that carries more evidence to their eyes.

The good news for believers is the opportunity to have a relationship with God and communicate with him. We communicate with God through prayer, meditation, and so forth. As a leader, you must learn and get used to pitching your tent and meeting with God (Exodus 33:7–11). That place of meeting is your place of encounter, your place of vulnerability, and it should never cease (1 Thessalonians 5:16–18; Luke 18:1).

Great leaders colead with God and maintain a flow of communication with him. They do not simply rely on their own knowledge; they get input and wisdom from God to know how to effectively lead the people entrusted to them. They turn to Him at the peak of their strength or their lowest moment (Philippians 4:6). Because they understand that whatever they need is hidden in the intimacy of their communication with God. King Solomon asked for wisdom; God gave it to him and added wealth, honor, and long life (1 Kings 3:4–15). Moses wanted reassurance as he stepped into his leadership role and God reassured him by confirming his presence with him (Exodus 33:12–19). Jacob needed an increase of supply, God showed him favor (Genesis 31:1–13). King David needed mercy and forgiveness after poor decision-making, he turned to God who showed mercy to him (Psalm 51; 86).

To our followers, we may be leaders, but to God, we are His followers. Hence, His leadership affects and molds us into His image and likeness (Genesis 1:26–28). We as leaders become the expression of His intention toward people as we embody the values of His leadership upon us. Do not just stop at the vertical communication, now engage in the horizontal communication, because leadership is not only "God and me," but also "God, His people, and me." We cannot be effective in our vertical communication if we fail at our horizontal communication (1 John 4:20).

Communication involves others. The truth is that strategic leadership is about involving people to create an outcome. Horizontal communication gives an effective tactic to leadership strategy which in turn must synchronously "influence individuals and the group as a whole, while changing power, identity, and meaning," Ackermann and Eden (2012, 19) wrote.

As a leader, you must always be "prepared to give an answer to everyone who asks you to give the reason for the hope that you have" (1 Peter 3:15 (NIV)). In other words, you must be able to explain and communicate to people why they should believe you and what you stand for.

The same way many wonder whether leaders are born or made, many ask if good communicators are born, or good communication is acquired through learning. We can learn from 1 Corinthians 14:9 that eloquence is not necessarily a good communication skill. One can eloquently speak without necessarily conveying an understandable and reliable message. After all, "if good communication skills were just common sense and eloquence, then communication would not so often go awry, and we would live in a world where misunderstanding rarely occurred" (Alberts, Nakayama, and Martin 2007, 4).

Let it be clarified now that effectiveness in communication is not in the abundance or rarity of words; your message must be plain and carriable. Take time to clearly convert your leadership message so that those who receive can interpret and run with it. In fact, Habakkuk 2:2 says, "Write my answer plainly on tablets, so that a runner can carry the correct message to others" (NLT).

If you ever survey great leaders that walk the path of earth, you will realize that, commonly, they knew how to communicate their vision and expectations with their followers. That mastery of communication did not happen in a day, they learned and enhanced it with years and experience. For instance, Apostle Paul, in 2 Timothy 2:2, took the time needed to clearly teach his leadership message to Timothy and asked him to also find reliable and faithful men that could continue with the mission. This is the same apostle that wrote the most books in the New Testament, and whose legacy is not left unnoticed. He understood that communication is the pillar of all forms of interactions in life. Ignoring such fact is setting oneself up for failure; caring for it is giving oneself the possibility to improve and succeed in leadership.

Since communication is a channel that carries a message from the sender to the receiver, it is undeniable that mastery of communication gives leaders a sense of confidence in who they are and gives their followers a sense of trust in who they are following. Just like with any other skills, a leader must constantly improve their communication skills.

There are several reasons why you as a leader should invest in improving your communication skills. Here are a few:

- Leaders should communicate effectively to improve and sustain their image of self.

- Leaders should improve their communication to meet social needs and build relationships.
- Leaders should learn to communicate to exchange information adequately.
- Leaders should know how to communicate to influence others.
- Leaders should improve their communication to build and maintain relationships.

According to Anderson and Adams (2016, 119), "everything happens in or because of a conversation." Moreover, every exchange is a potential moment of truth, a point of failure, or a critical link in the chain of success. For a leader, strategic communication guarantees that the impact of your message is consistent with your intention and results in understanding.

There are three critical components that aspiring leaders should seek for excellent communication, Baldoni (2005) believes:

1. the development of the leadership message,
2. the delivery of the leadership message,
3. the maintenance of the leadership message.

Most of those with poor communication skills can't sustain strong relationships with their followers. They struggle to adequately mature, deliver, and preserve their leadership message. This usually leads to leadership frustration because one feels misunderstood, and followers become confused because they struggle to grasp what is being communicated.

An environment that encourages communication is set to have less communication problems than the one who does not encourage. Just like the principle of reaping and sowing, whatever culture or behavior a leader allows in his or her relationship with his followers is more likely to be the basis of the relationship in the long run. As Burton, Obel, and Døjbak (2016, 276) say, "communication has to be in focus, not just to assure continued commitment but also to attend to delays and deal with their implications for the implementation plan." The Bible is indeed an unlimited resource that lays the foundation for proper leadership communication, whether it is interpersonal, intrapersonal, or extra-personal.

How to improve your communication skills based on biblical principles:

    a. Listen more than you speak.
    b. Value the receiver of the message as much as you value the message.
    c. Be aware of your nonverbal communication, especially your body language.
    d. Think through your message before making it known.
    e. Be concise.
    f. Learning to adequately communicate is a journey that never ends.

Chapter Seven

Building a Team

As iron sharpens iron, so one person sharpens another.
—*Proverbs 27:17 (NIV)*

For the Lord's portion is his people.
—*Deuteronomy 32:9 (NIV)*

Overcoming the challenge of creating a vision is a significant milestone in a leadership journey. However, it will serve no purpose if there is no team to carry it to success. As much as it is important to focus on having a vision, it is as crucial to bring people together to help run with the vision. Habakkuk 2:2 advises to "write the vision; make it plain on tablets, so he may run who reads it [a herald may run with it]" (NLT/NIV).

Many people are eager to lead yet neglect some of the basic laws that control or play a vital role in their ability to have, maintain, and multiply their team. Whether the leader and the follower are in North America, Asia, Europe, or Africa, the laws for team success are still the same—of course, with a slight adjustment based on the culture and values of the organized group. Apart from personality traits being among the global principles of success between leader-and-follower relationships, skill-approach plays an important role as well to the strengthening of a team.

A team represents the group of codependent people that come together to accomplish desirable common goals and secure valued rewards. Rothwell (2016, 4) believes that the most successful teams are made of members who "love working in groups and who experience the rewards." According to Northouse (2016), it is the vision's captivating nature that touches followers' experiences and pulls them into supporting the group. When a group has a clear vision, it is easier for people to learn how they fit in with the overall group and society. It inspires them because they feel they are a significant dimension of a worthwhile initiative.

Gathering a team is one of the first steps toward building a team. It is the leader's obligation to assign roles and responsibilities for proper management, functioning, and to avoid assumption and overlapping responsibilities. When God expressed His desire to team up with the nation of Israel, He made sure to also create a system of organization and structure that assign through His servants' positions and/or roles' description to each of the twelve groups, also known as families in Israel, (Genesis 49, 1–29; Deuteronomy 33). And even more specific to some of the appointed individuals within those tribes, such as Abraham to father a nation (Genesis 17:4-6), Solomon to build a temple (1 King 5:5, 1 Chronicles 28:6), Paul to be a representative to the gentiles (Acts 9:15), Isaiah to be His spokesman (Isaiah 6).

We see Jesus doing the same with his twelve disciples. As they were journeying with him, more and more description to their roles were added which was sealed by the common goal found in Matthew 28:18–20. For instance, Judas was known as the disciple in charge of the money bag (John 12:6), John was trusted with Jesus's mother (John 19:27), and Peter was being trained into a fisher of men and a key custodian of the kingdom of heaven (Matthew 4:19; Matthew 16:17–19).

While leaders play a role in communicating the vision, the vision's materialization derives from both the leader and the team. Woolfe (2019, 130) demonstrated that "people are a leader's most important asset," and the book of Deuteronomy 32:9 added that people are the Lord's portion. Despite all the resources available, each team member plays a crucial role in fulfilling the vision. Your team members serve as the builders of the walls to your vision. A leader as prominent as Jesus did not let his ability keep him away from working together with others. In fact, Matthew

4:18–21 and Mark 1:16–20 recount recruiting—or, as some would say, "team formation"—as one of Jesus's first leadership activities. The criteria upon which he picked them is not known. However, if we survey and study the Bible, we notice a reoccurrence of criteria leaders should look for that is also used throughout the Bible:

- Team members that could follow (Matthew 4:19; Luke 5:27)
- Members that carry or have the potential to carry the same mind-set (Genesis 2:20–23)
- Members whose agenda is the common goal, not personal agenda (Judges 7:1–6)
- Members who are ready to work toward the fulfillment of the vision (Nehemiah 3)
- Members who stay teachable (1 Peter 5:5; Proverbs 22:6)
- Members that believe in your leadership and in your vision (Hebrews 11:1)

Would the above criteria be effective if leaders did not understand the five steps to the team development process? Probably not, because each of those criteria unveils itself progressively as a team begins to spend some time together and the leader begins to read character and motives. It is often a source of frustration to leaders when they see the display of certain behaviors among their team members, and they may begin to resist the person instead of dealing with the behavior, like Jesus did with Peter (Matthew 16:23) and Judas (Matthew 26:25; John 12:3–8). Leaders need to understand the stages which their team is going through to know how to tackle some of the challenges that may arise.

Here are the five stages to the team-development process as proposed by Bruce Tuckman in 1965 that leaders should watch for:

1. Forming stage: At this stage, the leader usually shares the vision with the potential team members to get them on board with the common goal. When Gideon was tasked with defeating their oppressors, he came up with a team. This was the beginning of his team life, and all these men were probably excited to team up with Gideon, a man who had an encounter with the angel of God, a man who had a vision of victory (Judges 6:33–35, 7:1–8). Because they were in their honeymoon stage at that point, their interaction was still shallow, because they did not quite clearly understand the expectations and responsibilities it required to be on such a team.
2. Most of the men at this stage were testing the water and were not yet at the realm of conviction when it came to their desire to serve the common goal alongside Gideon. This was the same with the children of Israel when they were initially told about their deliverance from Egypt (Exodus 3:16–18). However, reality hit, and they started reevaluating their decision to join such a team. Indeed, after the honeymoon stage comes responsibility. Joining a team can be compared to marriage and marriage is not the party or when everyone is cheering and celebrating your decision to join hands; marriage is not the honeymoon — marriage is what comes after all the decoration, music, food, and guests are part of the memory. Marriage is the decision to take responsibilities for the common good and goal and stand by each other no matter what.
3. Storming stage: At this stage, things like character, potential apprehension, vision acceptance, and dissonance begin to unveil themselves in the

members. This stage is said to be the most challenging of all the stages because it is often a source of conflict and resistance—the team is going through a contrary wind while navigating differences and change. It should not be a surprise if some team members decide to leave the group, if a leader does not see fit to keep a member or if frustration and friction rises among members, and that includes the leader. If the forming stage is not well handled, the storming stage will directly lead to the adjourning stage, which will later be addressed in this chapter.

4. Clarify on expectations, roles, and responsibilities. Work hand in hand with your team to establish an acceptable way of doing and acting. Value them but do not forsake your position as a Christlike leader as well. Reassure them on the importance of their participation because each one of them is part of the team and all form the team. When needed, address behaviors that may, in the long run, hinder the team life while highlighting the values the team stands for. This is a good stage for the leader to remind the vision and mission and address any blind spots in the journey. The interactions at this stage help set the tone on how group members communicate which influences their satisfaction as well as productivity. If the forming stage is the honeymoon stage, then the storming stage can be equated as the "wilderness stage." The place where, as mentioned above, character, fear, and so forth is unveiled, an opportunity for the leader to speak from the heart, and to the heart of his team, and adequately "lead the ship" to quiet and safe waters.

5. Norming stage: Once a team learns to manage and

overcome challenges in the storming stage, it allows them to develop a better synergy. According to Garrison (2015), this is where the rift of expectations is enunciated. They learn to respect and accept each other's uniqueness, role, and create a group culture founded on established values and norms. The norming stage is the modus operandi of team building. It is one of a leader's biggest challenge to promote a healthy team-building opportunity within the group, so as to create a sense of oneness, cooperation, and easiness with little to no resistance to the team and its members.

6. At this stage, team members begin to embrace the leadership of the leader they believed in and grasp the concept of the vision they followed. Better than in the previous stages, their mind-set is now wired to accept the responsibilities and expectations it will take to reach the common goal and ensure a proper atmosphere within the group. This does not in any way mean that conflict and disagreement will never emerge again. It simply implies that if it is the case, the team will have an established and approved set of norms upon which to fall to help them bounce out of an eventual return into the storming stage.

7. Performing stage: Once the team has strengthened its interpersonal relationship and reached a more structured and hierarchized stage, the whole team is now eager and ready to start performing. This is where talent and talk meets motivation and birth the work. Each team member begins to tackle the mission creatively and innovatively as it is connected to their responsibilities and role within the team. At this stage, the leader can see a high

increase in team performance and commitment because members seem more focused, aligned, and purpose driven

8. Adjourning stage: As its title implies, this is the stage that ushers the team to its termination. This stage is usually tied to the storming stage. When conflict, disagreement, and miscommunications are not well handled, they begin to cripple the health of the team, sometimes to the point of creating unhealthy and unbalanced rivalry between members and between the members and the leaders.

9. It shouldn't be surprising to the leader to notice an increase of cliques and under-the-table conversations and plots. Trust is menaced because every morbid conversation or behavior is a spark of fire that has the potential to grow into a wildfire and scatter people away from the common goal. At this stage, one of the best ways to survive is to promote communication, healthy ones. As a leader, take the time to hear your team members. After all, they are the herald running with your vision. From the groundwork where they perform, they face a reality that you might not be aware of, which can influence their emotions, behavior, and apprehension of the team and your leadership.

10. Hear them and evaluate their input. Advise, confront, empower, encourage, and be intentional wherever needed, but do not ignore the red flags and play blind on the struggles in this stage. As if it has not been emphasized, prioritize communication, because what you choose to communicate or not to communicate as a leader produces a result and it better be deemed good. Although there is a place for valuing peace over confrontation when it

comes to addressing conflict, Garrison (2015) instructs that an efficient leader should not be conflict-averse because leadership is also dealing with the elephant in the room to preserve the group.

Moving forward, with the importance of building a team to succeed as a leader. It is crucial to remember that, despite the diverse and large quantity of creation around the man (Adam), his teammate (Eve) came from within him (Genesis 2:21–23). Those that need to be part of your team will even, at the least of percentage, carry a part of your DNA, because your leadership position is not only for you to get help but it is also for you to train up followers until they reach a maturity level that can make them contenders in leadership. At the proper time, you should be able to recognize the likeness in them. They will not be you, but uniquely be recognized as "bones of your bones and flesh of your flesh," such as in Acts 4:13–14 where it is written, "Now when they saw the boldness of Peter and John, and perceived that they were uneducated, common men, they were astonished. And they recognized that they had been with Jesus. But seeing the man who was healed standing beside them, they had nothing to say in opposition."

Looking at the large number of people that initially followed Gideon and Jesus are proof that a team is not built based on quantity but rather on quality. Using Colossians 4:7–17, I would like for us to agree that each team is made of at least these six types of individuals:

1. Members-brother: They stick through all and can be all types of members depending on the situation.
2. Members with common interests: They are only members because they see common interests or know common people.
3. Members-followers: The bond to this partnership

is the inspiration one is to the other. They do not hesitate to reach out when they need help and advice, and vice versa.
4. Distanced-members, or members at a distance: The only reason why they are still members is because there is this distance between them and the leader. Although they do not have direct access to the leader and may never get to speak often to the leader, they care for the vision and the team as if the leader was closer to them.
5. Members-helper: They are not necessarily waiting for you to do the same for them, but they are always willing to help you. Sometimes, even after you screw them.
6. Members-traitor: First occasion offered, they will betray and leave. The intensity of their involvement depends on seasons. Self-interest and hidden agendas often motivate them.

Belonging to a team or group is everyone's wish. Griffin (2015, 124–131) explained that Maslow placed that need at the center of all humans' desires in his hierarchy of needs in between psychological needs, safety needs, and self-esteem and self-actualization. However, no one wants to be part of a group of people led by someone they cannot relate to, someone who does not understand their role and identity. No one wants a leader that is not inspiring in his way of carrying himself and his way of treating his subordinates. No one wants a leader whose only agenda is self-centered at the expense of the team. Those are some of the least attractive qualities a leader can possess, and a follower can be attracted to. Always remember that your followers follow your ship so that your leadership leads their ships to better waters.

Chapter Eight

Invest in Building Relationships: Build Trust

Sovereign LORD, you are God! Your covenant is trustworthy, and you have promised these good things to your servant.
—2 Samuel 7:28 (NIV)

Then Jonathan made a covenant with David because he loved him as himself.
—1 Samuel 18:3 (NIV)

"Relationship" is one of the oldest, if not the oldest, forms of connection there can be. Oftentimes, when a leader spots potential, his first reaction is to want to invest in the potential to see how the potential can serve them. However, this kind of approach to the leadership and followership relationship always ends up frustrating some and creating a sense of abuse when the potential is not as effective as the leader wanted them to be. Or, as in the case of King Saul and David in 1 Samuel 18:17, the potential of the latter one begins to propel their reputation in the sight of men and causing jealousy and lack of trust from the leader.

Trust is not taught as a science, but it is inherently learned and earned through some kind of interaction. The best way to invest in leadership relationships is to build trust in the leader-follower relationship. Care and cater for the person more than you do to their gift. Give them the opportunity to be valued by you more than their gift is valued. Do not just ask about what they can do but try to find out how you can serve them so they can blossom in their gift and calling.

Saul and David's connection is a prime leader-follower relationship that was focused on the gift and not necessarily the person. Both Saul and David did not have enough time to genuinely build a strong relationship and mutual trust. David got into service because of the need of his musical skills in a time of spiritual oppression in the life of the king (1 Samuel 16:14–23). He later joined the king's camp because of his agility in the battlefield (1 Samuel 17:55–58, 18:5–16). Would they have developed a trust relationship? Maybe King Saul wouldn't have been intimidated by David's popularity? Trust is never static; it either evolves or regresses. It is environmental, and the culture of the environment is determined by the leader. David's rise should have been a proud moment for King Saul to witness because more than being about the individual, such explosion of potential pointed toward the quality of potential in the team.

On the other hand, all throughout his ministry we see Jesus engaging in building trust with the people around him. We particularly see it with the disciples and some of the people he encountered. Before Matthew 10 and the release of the ability to perform, there was Matthew 4 and the introduction of the followership relationship and the trust journey. That journey laid the foundation to the trust's circle of safety for his team and within his team.

Becoming a trusted person requires a lot more than an individual can think of because trust is not something that is learned in school or something that is transferable. Northouse (2016, 173) wrote, "Trust has to do with being predictable or reliable, even in situations that are uncertain." Trust is built with history and constant evaluation of the relationship; it takes time to build it but a fraction of a second to break it. Trust is the most important element of a team culture and without the safety circle of trust, people tend to overthink the negative consequences and engage in negative behaviors.

According to Maister, Green, and Galford (2000), motivated leaders spend great energy in refining and perfecting their skills and specific expertise while acquiring experience and expanding their knowledge and networking. However, rarely do "they give enough thought to creating trust relationships" (x). Leadership ultimately comes down to creating a condition of trust within the organization that sends a strong message of selfless service, not self-serving leadership.

The truth of the matter is, "trust is the vital bond that unifies leaders with their followers and research has shown that trust is about relationship. If leaders were better equipped to quickly build genuine trust with their followers, there would likely be a significant increase in effectiveness and efficiency" (Stubbendorff and Overstreet 2019, 15–16). Indeed, when a team evolves from within the safety circle of trust, it makes collaboration and communication less of a struggle.

Today's world is challenged by a crisis of trust. However, this crisis can be resolved if individuals learn to engage, lead, connect, serve, Samson (2018, 2) said. Trust in a relationship requires availability from both parties. It is reciprocated: you give, and you receive. Knowing that the other party is available in times of discouragement, fear, or needs creates a sense of safety and trust. It is measured by the involved parties' ability to be part of what is done.

When Joshua was fearful, God asked him to trust Him and be courageous because He was there with him (Joshua 1:9). Trust is what sustains relationship in a team. The sooner a leader promotes a culture of trust in a team, the faster members can begin to engage in it, because teamwork relies solely on human engagements to produce a desirable change.

Cummings and Worley (2010) explained that "the richness and validity of the information gathered will depend on the extent to which the leader develops a trust relationship with the group and listens to opinions" (127). They define trust as "a psychological state comprising the intention to accept vulnerability based upon positive expectations of the intentions or behaviors" (570). Trust is a characteristic of successful association, and generally, people get in partnerships with the hope to improve the relation's quality and leverage trust among the involved parties. It entails an expectation that the parties will put on the side their self-interest for the joint interest of the relationship under given conditions. As a leader, your role is to provide the "why" to the "what" and leave the how to your team members. This will help avoid micromanagement and nurture trust in their ability to achieve the common goal. Delegating decision-making to the whole team creates a virtuous circle of trust.

Hackman and Johnson (2013) added that patterns of trust, loyalty, and commitment in relationships are strongly influenced by the culture in which each party belongs and its values. In a trusting environment, individuals are more productive and enjoy better relationships and are willing to go beyond what is required or expected.

According to Kouzes and Posner (2004), it is essential to think about which values of the Christian faith are most crucial when establishing a relationship and building trust. Values such as integrity, authenticity, joy, and dignity of work can sustain the relationship. However, "trust comes down to what is between an individual and God" (97). Seeing people through God's perspective helps in building trust, and trusting God helps in becoming a trustful person.

The books 1 Samuel 20 and 2 Samuel 9 summarize the above statement as it relates the story of the covenant between two friends, David and Jonathan, who trusted in the Lord as the bond of their relationship. This empowered their relationship and allowed them to stay accountable to their covenant. Power comes in several types, one of which is the power of relationship which has to do with the close associations a person has with a variety of people (Bellman 2002).

When a relationship is nurtured, and trust is birthed, both parties feel at ease with each other and are ready to take a risk and accept change. However, none of that would be possible outside of a form of communication. The truth is, "effective messages are built upon trust, which is demonstrated in thought, word, and deed. Such a message is rooted in the character of the individual as well as his or her place within the relationship" Baldoni (2005, xi–4) explained.

According to Muehlhoff and Lewis (2010, 110), trust is a foundational trait of healthy communication climates and relationships and "a lack of trust can be deeply problematic for communication when it becomes the interpersonal norm, rather than an occasional response." Ephesians 4:25 and Colossians 3:9 are excellent examples of a situation where effective communication was threatened by mistrust, dishonesty, and lack of integrity. Paul's strategy to rebuild trust was to encourage truthfulness, honesty, which Ciulla (2014) presents as "a set of specific practical and moral obligations and is a necessary condition for empowerment." Concerning honesty, Proverbs 11:3 says, "The integrity of the upright shall guide them: but the perverseness of transgressors shall destroy them" (KJV). Throughout the Bible, God points toward His unfailing character, not just to connect with His creation but also encourage trust in Him. Because He is faithful (1 Cor. 10:13), light (1 John 1:5), patient (2 Peter 3:9), just (Hebrews 4:12), loving (John 3:16), etc., He should be trusted.

The point is so people can always rely on Him, even in the midst of vulnerability. As a team, relying on others in a time of vulnerability can strengthen the relationship and stir compassion toward one another. In fact, Galatians 6:2 advises bearing one another's burdens. This requires encouraging communication, collaboration, and accountability.

Kouzes and Posner (2004, 28) explained that the legend of the hero leader that does all by themselves is not true. Leaders build trust by fostering collaboration, by the example they set and by listening actively. "Followers will only take ownership of their work when there is enough trust within the organization, and without trust, they will be hesitant to make decisions for fear of possible retaliation," Hackman and Johnson (2013, 117) said.

Integrity is another brick to the wall of trust and is known to be of critical spiritual value. According to Northouse (2016, 25), "integrity is the quality of honesty and trustworthiness. People who adhere to a strong set of principles and take responsibility for their actions are exhibiting integrity. They are loyal, dependable, and not deceptive." Concerning integrity, Proverbs 4:25–27 says to concentrate on what is essential and not lose focus.

Life is made of ever-changing cycles, and change means risk-taking. Bellman (2002, 74–77) wrote, "Risk-taking requires trust, and for trust to be built, there must be a relationship. However, although a relationship does not take away change and risk-taking, building trust can make risk and change more acceptable." Establishing trust is an ability transformational leaders hold because they understand that trust gives the group a sense of integrity equivalent to a healthy identity (Northouse 2016). This is something that is seen throughout the Bible with God in His relationship with human beings. Oftentimes when He covenanted with people, He gave them the guarantee of His presence and His participation even in times of uncertainty.

Although there is a crisis of trust in today's world, biblical evidence, such as those found in the book of Exodus, shows that people are always looking for a person they can trust and lean on for a glimpse of hope. This brings out the fact that trust involves emotions and demands some level of emotional intelligence. The acknowledgment that emotions are essential in decision-making and trust-building, such as in instances of dealing with risky assets, is progressively growing. Emotional states such as fear and the enjoyable feeling of relief from fear could manifest themselves in the valuation and risk assessments of choice options, Van Well and Van Winden (2019) explained.

People follow leaders because they believe and hope to find wisdom and inputs that may unlock their growth and maybe save their work (Biech 2011). Proverbs 11:14 says, "Where there is no guidance, a people fall, but in an abundance of counselors, there is safety" (ESV). There is an interdependence that makes the relationship process everybody's responsibility. Block (2011) reported that "when each is responsible for the learning of the whole, then each share a deeper sense of purpose with all; accepting this demands cooperation and a willingness to acknowledge our connectedness" (311).

As previously said, one of the fundamental roles of a leader is to build trust with his or her followers in order to maintain a healthy relationship. Lack of trust is one of the four fundamental objections and an active area of resistance that may prevent a leader from having a healthy relationship with his or her followers. According to Lingenfelter (2009), relationship and community are fundamental to the life and work of the community, and the first task in establishing relationships is building trust within a bond. Truth is, concentrating on building mutual trust is vital because trust is the bond that sustains the relationship between both parties. Trust is one of the global principles of mastering the leader-follower relationship. People follow someone whose skills are attractive to them but stay loyal to a leader they can trust. It is good to note that "building a close relationship early in the process is crucial because it will make the difficult conversations later in the process productive" (Block 2001, 221).

Trust is also strengthened when leaders encourage a culture of collaboration, creativity, productivity, accountability, and foster the proper attitude with their followers. When both parties begin to share the same cultural values, they learn to trust and become accountable to each other. Accountability empowers authenticity. Responsibility and authenticity help maintain a balance in the group's life. According to Squires (2003), partners who work well together could multiply efficiently and improve the bottom line because "cooperation opens doors and smooths operations" (55).

We see in the Old and New Testaments how the different use of communication and the enforcement of integrity caused the rapid expansion of faith around the world and the maintenance of peace in Israel. Many stories prove how Jesus engaged in those trust-building relationships with his disciples by using strategies such as introducing himself, vision sharing, etc.

Every time Paul brought a solution to an occurring situation, he made sure it was communicated adequately to the masses and that his audience understood that they were accountable to each other (1 Corinthians 1:1–10). Paul knew how to control his feelings and the emotion of the crowd which inspired trust in return (Panait 2017). He also had some leadership ability and cultural knowledge, also known as insider knowledge, (Acts 2:13–14) that helped him address his audience with regard to their cultural setting, Robins (1996) says.

According to Kouzes and Posner (2004), "trust is built when leaders make themselves vulnerable to other people whose subsequent behavior they cannot control" (89). One of the fascinating yet challenging leadership journeys was that of Moses and the children of Israel. How could they trust a leader they may have not had previous relationship with? He was Aaron and Miriam's brother, but his upbringing was nothing like that of the children of Israel. He grew up in the luxury of the oppressors of the Israelites, and suddenly he was to be their liberator?

How could Moses be trusted with so many lives outside of Egypt while he turned his back on the Egyptians who "gave him" life? Although these questions were never raised to object his leadership, we can agree that the relational challenges that rose between Moses as a leader and the children of Israel point toward an unsolidified bond of trust among them.

When a leader lacks confidence in the vision, it is indirectly and, sometimes, directly projected to the followers. According to Woolfe (2019), "adversity can quickly stop a leader who lacks purpose, but it only fans the flames of a leader with a strong purpose" (48). When a group or a leader believes in a purpose, they do not look for a back door or side door to escape when things get rough.

When Moses finally had a grasp of his purpose as a leader, his first reaction was to doubt (Exodus 3), not because it was impossible but more so because it was bigger than him, and he could not fathom in his mind how he could be a carrier of such magnificent vision. Chapters later, the writing in the Exodus book displayed the different occurrences of doubt within that group. Every time adversity rose, they seemed to doubt the vision and lose trust in the visionary.

Conflict within a group may be an indication of a lack of trust between members of a group. Forty years through the wilderness seems like forty years of conflict-resolution attempts. There were conflicts with outsiders (Exodus 6), within the leadership team (Exodus 12), and conflict within the group. According to Stubbendorff and Overstreet (2019, 15–18), trust is about a relationship. Leaders need a relationship with their followers to influence them. Simultaneously, "a leader's trust in followers makes the leader more open to their influence" (Stubbendorff and Overstreet 2019, 16).

It can be disputed that trust was such a big issue in Moses's leadership because Moses was on the competitors' side (the Egyptians). However, when he finally discovered his vision, he switched teams. That action by itself could have dug a hole in the foundation of trust between him and the Egyptians. He joined a team with whom he initially might not have built any relationship and suddenly got appointed to a leadership position while there were probably people waiting in line for that very same opportunity. According to Kouzes and Posner (2004), "the degree to which a leader builds trust affects the kind of organization they grow. Furthermore, ultimately, this is where it all starts and stops with a leader" (97).

Part Three
How Some Leaders Failed

Chapter Nine

Lack of Ethical Leadership

*Whoever conceals his transgressions will not prosper,
but he who confesses and forsakes them will obtain mercy.*
—*Proverbs 28:13 (ESV)*

*Show yourself in all respects to be a model of good works,
and in your teaching show integrity, dignity.*
—*Titus 2:7 (ESV)*

Although many envy leadership positions, some have come to the realization that it is a slippery slope position that can make or break a person if one ignores the ethical signals on his journey. How can we talk about leadership and ignore the ethical aspect of leadership? How can we dive into the relationship between ethics and leadership if we do not begin by properly defining ethics?

What Is Ethics?

Ethics is to leadership what the heart is to a human being, and no leader can reach their full development without it. According to Ciulla (2014, 4), "leadership entails a distinctive kind of human relationship with distinctive sets of moral problems." It is essential to know that what attracts people to each other is not merely the position they hold or the connection they have but also the character they portray and the value they support. Even better, people identify with groups based on the ethics they share, see in them, and the added value they hope to gain from associating themselves with the group.

Northouse (2016, 330) defined ethics as "the kinds of values and morals an individual or society finds desirable or appropriate," that influence what they do and who they are. In other words, ethics is the morality behind a human's action. Hence their actions are an indication to what they value. It is developed in three stages, also known as the Kohlberg's stages of moral development: (1) preconventional morality, (2) conventional morality, and (3) post-conventional morality.

In the quest for preserving and protecting human lives and society, the fundamental human interests must be defended. Each person is expected to hold a certain standard of ethics for the well maintenance of society. God in his sovereignty established the standard of ethics for humankind by giving him the choice to choose (Genesis 2:9–17). The Bible talks about the tree of the knowledge of good and evil, the simple fact of eating from that tree causes death. What if, as human beings and leaders, we all have that tree planted in the secret gardens of our lives and are responsible in our choice of eating of it was a command preestablished in eternity? As a leader, you have the responsibility and duty to make the choice. It is that choice that will either give life or death to your leadership journey, (Deuteronomy 30:15–20.)

As time is evolving and history is being made, a greater sense of ethics is growing in people in reaction to all the happenings. To be known as an ethical leader or a leader that has reached the full leadership development range, one needs to portray behaviors that set a positive standard to those around them. Many people assert knowing ethics based on their experience yet fail to properly grasp the depth of ethics.

For leadership, ethics is a responsibility to assume, a priority to maintain, an opportunity to snatch, and boundaries to protect. Ethics is the principle of choice and balance; it is made of beliefs and consequences that dictate human behavior in favor of good and right decisions. In leadership, it plays a proactive role of raising awareness on the responsibility and priority of each, while being an opportunity to make a difference and a boundary that creates the proper knowledge and protection against unethical behavior and its consequences.

1) **Responsibility**

Ethics is every leader's responsibility because it is at the core of your success as a leader. For many theorists out there, responsibility is the most relevant dimension of the ethical matters that confront leaders (Ciulla 2014). The sooner you accept that responsibility, the quicker you can start working on your understanding and valuing your role as an ethical agent in leadership. It may sound like an easy task to do; however, it is not as evident as it seems for many people. In fact, Franklin (2020, 34) commented that an individual flourishes through the human lifespan and a continuing "process of negotiating biological and sociocultural forces. Humans must successfully reconcile these conflicting forces and achieve the trait or virtue of each stage." Until then, they will still work through the tests of ethics, as they evolve in their ethical journey.

When God created man, He empowered him with the capacity to make ethical choices based on the standard established (Genesis 2:16–17). Adam and Eve later failed at that test and refused to take any responsibility of their unethical behavior and engaged themselves in the blaming game, forsaking any personal and mutual accountability. As a human being, and especially a leader, your ethical knowledge is always tested, there is always that inner voice causing you to question what you know as the standard of good and evil. It is your responsibility to shut that voice down and stand on what you believe is the truth. A leadership built on unethical behaviors and decisions is a failed leadership, and time will tell on it.

2) **Priority**

The preservation of ethics should be a leader's number one priority, without which his whole leadership may fail and fall into a confusion of values. Once the ethics are understood, the values are shared, the decision-making and culture of the team are affected. Ethical decision-making over temporary comfort or success should always be the way to choose. Judas, the disciple in charge of Jesus's ministry finance (John 12:6, 13:29), was caught by greed and envy. These caused him to lose track of what was supposed to be his priority (John 12:5), and an ethical test like that of money and possessions' stewardship exposed what was really in his heart, the motive that drove his daily action (Matthew 26:14–16, 27:1–10; John 6:70–71). This is a great reminder to every believer, especially Christian leaders, to pay close attention to the things that have your attention. They most often create in you the intention that leads to your action. However, it is your responsibility to make sure those intentions do not cross out the boundaries of ethical decision-making.

Ethical leadership is not only with finance, but it also involves all aspects of a leader's life. Their public and private life interchangeably affects the outcome of each other. To date, most of the biggest leadership scandals involve sexual misconduct, greed, jealousy, and so forth. These scourges have risen around the world and affected people of all walks of life. More and more people are exposing or being exposed. Now, it is important to note that this is not a new wave; however, there seems to be an increasing number of people standing up against immoral sexual behavior in a society filled with selfish and negligent individuals who are egocentric and may think of themselves as exempted of all forms of ethics.

Most of them confessed to getting their priorities mixed up, thus affecting what they value and hurting the people that believed and supported them. Whether it happened in an open space or behind four walls, do not compromise your leadership journey for a temporary satisfaction that can divide and destroy what you are trying to build.

King David thought for a second that he could have gotten away with his sexual misconduct and murder; little did he know that, though men did not see him, the justice of God was lurking (2 Samuel 11:27, 12) and it was just a matter of time until a judgment fell on his kingdom (2 Samuel 12:10–14). Unethical decision-making does not only affect the leader but the whole team as well. Leaders should never ignore the red flags when they feel tempted into a misconduct. The price they have paid to get to where they are is far greater and more valuable than the consequences they will face.

In the quest of reaching the collective vision, it is up to the leader to influence the dos and don'ts within the parameters of the group. Although ethical leadership focuses for most of the time on the leader, it is acceptable to say that it also deals with the behaviors of the team because members of a team will act on the ethical values they were taught or which were allowed within the group. The common practice that members of a group exhibit come from the continuous transfer of norms and expectations among individuals.

3) Boundaries

There are no new scandals, just new people committing old outrages. Although we will go deeper on the topic of boundaries in leadership in Chapter 10, there are several aspects of leaders' behavior that play a crucial role in the implementation of ethical rules within groups, one of which is boundaries. Austin et al. (2006) and Doel et al. (2010), stated that "boundary" is a structure defined as the edge's demarcation of the proper behavior that clarifies what exists and what does not in the relationship between two entities. In other words, boundaries are made of what we create and allow in the relationship with others and ourselves. If our relationship with ourselves or others is a property, then boundaries are the walls that protect and define its value.

Concerning boundaries, Proverbs 25:17 advises believers to know their limits and avoid stepping on other people's ground for peace's sake. This means that though the possibility may be given to cross the boundaries established, one should choose not to do so to preserve the good health of the relationship. Ethical boundaries are essential, not just for others but for yourself because the second an individual begins to feel entitled to do what is pleasing to them because of a particular privilege, they risk stepping out of the boundaries established and corrupt their values and endanger their reputation and, to the extreme, their lives.

Once on the other side of the boundaries, people tend to notice that the appealing and envied green grass appearing beyond the borders is not as green as they thought. Instead, it is a dark place that traps and drains out what is left of the good reputation of the offender while putting everyone in danger and in an uncomfortable situation.

As it was said before, ethics is seen not just as a reaction to permanent consequences but also as an asset that protects one from experiencing consequences. Although consequences of unethical behaviors cannot always be avoided, through the several examples stated above, it is noticeable that once a leader engages in unethical decision-making, they risk the possibility of jeopardizing everything they built.

The Power of Decision-Making in Ethical Leadership

Northouse (2019) wrote that decision-making depends on the ethics held and shared by individuals or groups, which is either implicit or explicit. According to Kul (2017), ethical people are universally known for possessing values such as reliability, impartiality, and justice, which they implement through two-way communication with themselves (intrapersonal) and their audience (interpersonal) (Peng and Cheng 2016, 1256). Puka (2005) reveals that "morality grows in human beings spontaneously alongside physical limbs, basic mental and social capacities" (18). For this reason, leaders should nurture their ethical mind-set, so it guides their decision-making. When King David sinned (2 Samuel 12), Prophet Nathan did not hesitate one second before presenting to him what was the ethical way of dealing with his behavior. Even though David was king, he had to suffer the consequences of his unethical decision-making. This shows that ethical behavior concerns everybody, even leaders, and not just a group of people.

Mature ethical people such as Nathan, the Prophet, (1) understand that all lives matter and everybody has natural or unchallengeable rights and liberties established earlier than society, and it's everybody's duty to preserve that by making ethical decisions; (2) they see injustice as a violation of human rights and a counterproductive approach to development and fulfillment. They are entirely against the idea that individual egoistic well-being should contravene societal freedom.

A real ethical leader, then, does not look at his position as an opportunity to improve his lifestyle, but instead as a reason to transform the nation to "what good society should be like" (Northouse 2016, 332) without suppressing the freedom of thought from its subjects. Akbar, Khanam, et al. (2017) pointed that a nation is more likely to grow and cultivate relations when its people practice ethical morals in their decisions and judgment.

As Bishop (2013) explained, ethics becomes a preventative measure, protecting people and organizations from acting in harmful ways to this end; developing greater virtue, character, and responsibility in people and organizations significantly helps, according to the virtue ethics approach. Genesis 1:27–30 shows choice as the measure of ethical decision-making. Regardless of what an individual can be taught or asked to do, it is left to them to make an ethical choice when facing a decision. Personal values guide individuals' decisions and choices. Hultman and Gellermann (2002) believed that through the lens of values, people rank the importance of their decision and behavior to meet their needs.

The Sermon on the Mount presents an ethics based on the kingdom of heaven (Fedler 2006). Both the Sermon on the Mount and Plain are a collection of Jesus's teachings and personalized value system found in Matthew 5:1–14 and Luke 6:17–49. It defies the "institutional logic" form of self-absorbed leadership and raises the bar from self-focused leadership to servant-based leadership (Fedler 2006).

In this message, Jesus reveals several ethical concepts of servant-based leadership that challenge the "institutional logic" organizational system, Ciulla (2014) mentions. They include humility, concern for others, self-discipline, pursuing what's right, giving mercy toward people, leadership honesty and transparency, making peace rather than keeping it.

Unlike the "structural restraints" present in many of today's leaders, Jesus's view of ethics values what is respectable and relational. This sermon teaches us that ethics should be both respectable and relational. Respectable ethical leadership honors the time, energy, and work of their followers. Controneo (2015) calls it "relational ethics" and notes that since relationships demand our attention, relational trust, experience, and knowledge are fused into dynamics of ethical leadership. Randall (2012) develops the concept of relational ethics further by offering constructive incentives to reward followers. His research shows the use of legitimate ethical power that builds relational respect between leaders and followers. This is what Jesus was trying to model for us in the Sermon on the Mount. If our ethical approach is neither respectable nor relational then we must question the type of "structural restraints" that we are presenting to our followers.

What Is Then the Relationship between Ethics and Leadership?

It is good to note that no matter the type of leadership one is portraying or how ethical one believes they are as leaders, if it is not serving the greater good of the team and society at large then its ethical aspect should be questioned (Northouse 2016). This is all part of ethical integrity since it deals with "what is right, wrong, good, evil, virtue, duty, obligation, rights, justice, fairness, and responsibility in human relationships with each other and other living things" (Ciulla 2014, 4).

Poulfelt and Olson (2018) placed integrity at the center of the idea of professionalism and excellence. They explained that "integrity cannot be judged by what one says, only by that which they always do and make it nonnegotiable minimum standards" (40). Like the principle of reaping and sowing, whatever culture and behavior a leader allows is more likely to be the basis of the relationship in the long run.

According to Northouse (2016, 25), "integrity is the quality of honesty and trustworthiness. People who adhere to a strong set of principles and take responsibility for their actions are exhibiting integrity. They are loyal, dependable, and not deceptive." Concerning integrity, Proverbs 4:25–27 says to concentrate on what is essential and not lose focus. Cloud (2006) added that to not lose focus, a successful person needs to invest in mastering their craft.

Indeed, a leader's character is linked to his conduct. There is nothing beneficial about dishonesty, even when it sounds appealing. Berenbeim (2017) emphasized that integrity is the acknowledgment that the means employed are as crucial as the outcomes they achieve. Because integrity in solving ethical dilemmas necessitates a process that emphasizes on "the truth and accuracy of facts and the humility to acknowledge that the most important decisions are those that are made where the facts are incomplete or in dispute" (22).

History has proven that the practice of unethical leadership can have destructive results on the followers, the team in general, the leader, as well as the outsiders. Lewis (1952) explained that there are two ways in which the human goes wrong. One is when individuals "drift apart from one another, or else crash with one another and do one another damage, by cheating or bullying. The other is when things go wrong inside the individual when the different parts of him either drift apart or interfere with one another" (71). Northouse (2013) demanded leaders be authentic in their way of leading. He stated real and genuine leadership is about "the authenticity of leaders and their leadership. The authenticity of leadership is both an interpersonal practice (the relationship between leader and follower) and intrapersonal process (what goes on within the leader). Although the intersection between leadership and ethics remains a vast topic, as Christian believers and leaders we must agree that the standard of ethics is found in the written word of God.

It is known that perfection is not human, as Ecclesiastes 7:20 explains, and anyone who has such thought of himself or herself is "unaware of the gap between how ethical they think they are and how ethical they truly are" (Bazerman and Tenbrunsel 2011, 2). As a believer, it is vital to know that our standard for ethics is not established by our intentions, self-perception, or our satisfaction, instead by our obedience to God and His word (Luke 22:42).

No human being has flawless ethics. One can be people's favorite (1 Samuel 18:7), or a man after God's own heart (1 Samuel 13:14), yet fail at observing the fundamental ethical rules established by God's word. That is why it is always recommended to self-check our attitude and motive and pay close attention to the blind spots that may be threatening our ethics.

In a vehicle, blind spots are the side areas around the car that can't be easily seen unless the driver physically turns to observe and consider the situation. A lack of consideration of what is hidden in the blind spots may cause the car to get into an accident with the unspotted objects or even cause the driver and all passengers involved to lose their life.

Blind spots here represent the negative perceptions and behaviors an individual hold yet that is not taken into consideration. It comes from the partial attention people show to ethics (Pittarello, Leib, Gordon-Hecker, and Shalvi 2015). Only a leader who is aware of his or her blind spots can positively improve his/her behavior (Bazerman and Tenbrunsel 2011).

What example had David set by the killing of his best soldier for a short time of pleasure? Surely no one can plant a seed of an apple and expect mango to grow from that tree. He took one man's wife in secret but, as a fatal consequence, his illegitimate son's life was taken away and one of his sons publicly shamed all his concubines.

As a believer and a leader, the best reaction after unethical decision-making or behavior is not denial but confession/acknowledgment and rectification of the wrongdoings in the hope to reduce or attenuate the damage. Unethical behavior can destroy credibility and coldly estrange one another with no desire for reconciliation.

When standing on the roof and admiring the beauty of Bathsheba, David knew that his intentions were deceitful, yet engaged in self-serving justification to encourage his action (2 Samuel 11:1–2). He forgot that as a human being, a believer, and leader, he was not exempt from accountability. He was accountable to God and others. To God because His word is the foundation of our standard, and to others because they look up to us and trust us with their lives. Ethics demands to acknowledge others' existence and value and respect them for that despite their position, and our shared existence obliges us to repetitively make decisions, be they good or bad, about "what we ought to do" regarding others (Ciulla 2014, 33).

Building on the story in this chapter, some of the efficient ways of dealing with the temptation of behaving unethically or making an unethical decision are to acknowledge the temptation, evaluate the intention, then seek help if needed from trusted and mature people, pray, and ask God to help you overcome that temptation. Stay away from anything that can accentuate your desire to behave unethically.

According to Bazerman and Tenbrunsel (2011), a moral awareness of the temptation will cause a moral judgment of the situation which will influence the moral intention and bring about moral action. None of the above moral ability will be effective without a decent level of ethical self-awareness, which helps in understanding and accepting the limitations of the human mind and the blind spots it may produce.

Being ethical also means watching over one's heart and motive, as Proverbs 4:23 says. For Poulfelt and Olson (2018), people do not realize that a minor compromised character might hurt the future of their journey. In fact, "overlooking ethical violations can be debilitating and alienating to those who are more likely to witness violations of ethical policy" (63). Indeed, ethics is a crucial aspect of any leadership type, especially leadership in today's society.

The book of 2 Kings 5:20–17 shares the story of a mentee who faced an ethical financial situation. Greed got into him, and he wanted to charge a client for a service rendered free by his mentor, Elisha. Gehazi's unethical behavior caused him to lose his credibility in the sight of those that value him and miss on an opportunity to be elevated in due time. A lesson to learn from the story is that people are watching actions more than listening to words. The book of 1 Peter 2:12 recommends keeping our conduct honorable. No unethical action is worth jeopardizing your life and reputation. There is nothing beneficial about dishonesty, even when it sounds appealing. In short, successful ethical leadership looks like saying no to:

- Divisive leadership (Jeremiah 23:14; 2 Tim 2:24),
- Wicked leadership (Proverbs 16:12; Colossians 3:23–25; Proverbs 29:2),
- Morally corrupted leadership (1 Tim. 3:15),
- Misinformed leadership (Proverbs 29:6),
- Greedy leadership (Proverbs 16:18; Ezekiel 34:1–8), and
- Leadership without accountability (Hebrews 13:17; Acts 20:28).

Chapter Ten

Lack of Boundaries in Leadership

*Let what you say be simply "Yes" or "No";
anything more than this comes from evil.*
—Matthew 5:37 (ESV)

Do not move an ancient boundary stone set up by your ancestors.
—Proverbs 22:28 (NIV)

We slightly touched on the topic of boundaries when we wrote about the topic of ethics. We now have, through this chapter, the opportunity to elaborate more on the principles of boundaries as it pertains to Christian leadership. Boundaries is to leadership what pedals are to a car. It allows the drivers to know when to accelerate, reduce speed, or brake at all. As the driver of such vehicles, it is every leader's daily responsibility to care, use, and apply them. Boundaries are relation-based, and we owe it to ourselves and others for the preservation and well-running of our society. Boundaries come from the understanding of our role as ethical agents in our environment. Once you start accepting that the application of ethics is not only for others, you will also begin to ponder upon the boundaries by which you must live.

As a Christian leader, it is crucial to grasp the biblical perspective of boundaries, lest you want to experience what it feels like to drive down on a cliff with broken brake pedals. Understanding biblical principles on boundaries is the first step toward creating boundaries for a better leadership experience and avoiding revolt and resistance among team members. The second step is implementing them and making sure everyone within the scope of our influence performs from within the boundaries established, and if there is an instance of fence crossing, it is still a responsibility to correct the mistake by taking appropriate actions.

Cloud (2013) explained that not all boundaries work for all leaders; however, they should all seek to implement boundaries in the areas within the parameters of their leadership in the team to increase high performance, accountability, and results. Those areas are, but not limited to:

- the self,
- the vision and activities of the team,
- the relationship climate,
- the psychological environment: thought process, beliefs, and value culture,
- authority and responsibilities,
- performance and accountability.

These areas point toward the kind of healthy boundaries leaders should seek to establish and are summed up in:

- Boundaries in relationships with yourself and others
- Boundaries in relationships with work
- Boundaries in relationships with goods

Knowing our boundaries and implementing them are two very distinctive challenges for us to overcome as leaders. When it comes to limits in life there are two kinds of people: on the one hand, you have those that did not know boundaries existed or those that knew they needed boundaries but never set them, and on the other hand, those that knew their limitations and made sure all respected it. Just as the Bible advises on several leadership principles, it is also filled with examples of leaders that knew and didn't know how to implement boundaries. Whichever the case it was, both parties lived the consequences of the presence or lack of barriers in their leadership. And today we can take their lives as lessons for our lives.

1) The Self and Others vs. Boundaries

Being a leader doesn't mean having the right to do anything at any time without fear of the consequences. The Bible talks about leaders such as King David who endured loss and disaster for a boundary that was broken in secret (2 Samuel 11–12); King Saul died because he broke the limit of his authority because of pride and despair (1 Samuel 28); Judas suffered regret and was cursed because of the boundary of trust he broke (Matthew 27:1–10); Jezebel died a shameful and violent death (2 Kings 9:30–37); Lucifer suffered rejection because of the boundaries he trespassed; and so many more. Now, imagine if Jesus did not set the proper boundaries with Satan when he was tempted. Imagine if Jesus did not stand by the truth he knew and the value he held.

The area of our strength is most often the area we as humans and leaders tend to neglect because we feel like we have mastered it; hence, we do not need to keep an eye on it. A myth that has led many astray. Your area of strength and power should be monitored closely just as you do any other areas. Build secured fences around your strength and do not let foreign or past habits break in and weaken you. Peter was one of Jesus's most promising disciples, yet when Jesus declared praying for his disciples, he emphasized the prayer for Peter. Certainly, he knew that strength could become a weakness if taken for granted (Luke 22:31–34).

As a leader, you build and maintain boundaries around yourself through prayer and by keeping yourself accountable. As the Bible says, do not lean on your own understanding (Proverbs 3:5–6). You have probably heard people say, "trust your gut," but be challenged today to not lean on your gut only, because it may be subject to your preconceived goal and lustful desire.

In 1 Kings 11:3, the Bible talks about one of the wisest and wealthiest kings established over Israel at that time: Solomon. As a leader, he trespassed many of the boundaries that were created within his kingdom, thus causing him to not live by the well-known ethical values of the nation he led. Solomon got so comfortable with his wisdom that he did not counsel himself on the danger of having multiple partners from different and clashing beliefs. Solomon was the wisest man there was in his time, yet a lack of proper boundaries in his relationship with the opposite sex led him to destruction and an uncommon end of his leadership journey.

According to Moore (2017, 79), leadership is a risky path where the possibility of failure is astronomically high when a leader does not fully take responsibility of his journey: "The best way to avoid the leadership pitfalls of disqualifying failure is to become laser-focused on finishing well."

Mordecai saw the red flags around the fences of his relationship with Haman and established, from the get-go, the needed boundaries with Haman, even though the latter did not approve nor appreciate it (Esther 3). Everyone is entitled to their feelings, and no one should be forced to operate in an atmosphere where they feel psychologically threatened or manipulated. By birth, Esau was an established leader over his brother; however, for lack of psychological boundaries, he compromised himself and gave away his leadership for a bowl of soup (Genesis 25:29–34). Many leaders saw their leadership position taken away from them because of compromise or because they let someone else who seemed to have some influence over them manipulate their actions.

A good lesson to learn here is that your calling as a leader is to lead, serve, and empower others, not to be a people pleaser and do everything, even the things that go against your values, just so you can be approved by the few. It is interesting to note here that whether it was Mordecai who did not bow down to Haman and the rest of the Jews did, when the sentence of death came, it was extended to all. Here again, we see prayer as one of the outlets that helped preserve not only the lives of a people but the boundaries that were threatened by a leader's egocentric desire (Esther 8).

Pressure has led many leaders to disregard the reality of the barriers around the scope of their power and authority. Again, leadership is not a people-pleasing position. In fact, the power of leadership is in mastering the dynamics of relationships. After all, leadership is a personal process that caters to the followers' needs in order to fulfill the shared goal.

Pilate, a Roman leader, was sought after in the case of Jesus versus the people (Matthew 27:1–32). He didn't have enough evidence against Jesus to condemn him. However, because of the pressure he received from the priests and the population, he ended up taking a decision he did not necessarily agree with and later regretted, which was crucifying an innocent and releasing a guilty criminal (John 18:28–40). To avoid the pressure of his environment, Pilate failed to abide by the boundaries of integrity. Pilate allowed himself, out of a state of conformity and likability, to be dependent on outside pressure instead of ethically dealing with the matter at hand. This exposed the flaws in his character because he did not have the moral "ability to meet the demands of reality" (Cloud 2006, 24).

Leaders should never side with people in times of conflict; they should always be on the side of truth and justice as it is applied to their ethics. On several occasions, people expected Jesus's leadership to solve conflicts that he wasn't necessarily part of to begin. His wisdom caused him to actively settle disputes within the parameters of the complaint rather than stirring controversy by supporting one of the parties (Mark 10:35–45; John 8:1–11). As a leader, conflict resolution should not be about who you support; rather, it should focus and remain within the boundaries of the truth and righteousness.

This to say that no one, regardless of the opportunity at hand, should overlook and cross their self-boundaries for temporary satisfaction or pressure of any form. Always remember that credibility and integrity are at the foundation of any effective and efficient leadership.

2) Boundaries in Relation with Work

Effective leadership is not overworking yourself at the cost of your existence. Work hard and smart but do not become slaves to work. The system in which we live in society has convinced us that effectiveness is in staying busy. However, it can be a rebuttal because busyness is not equal to efficiency. When Pharaoh wanted to punish the children of Israel for "thinking and planning," he multiplied their work, reduced help to keep them busy (Exodus 5). You as a leader should think of ways you can work and delegate work where and when needed. Your leadership work should not become a taskmaster that imposed a slave-like lifestyle on you. You build healthy fences around work in your leadership by following these four principles found in Genesis 1:

1. Taking responsibility of the work you must do as a leader means not leaving all the work to your team while simply enjoying the benefits of being at the top. Real leaders get their hands dirty and become models of inspiration to their team. How would you appreciate the result of the shared goal if you did not partake in the process of its realization? Having a goal of how things ought to be is great but getting an understanding of the ins and outs is even better. Uncommon experiences will only come down if you as a leader take part in what is being built. Solomon's involvement caused the Israelites, especially the leaders to all the families, to experience, to a greater dimension, a glory they have probably only heard of and never personally experienced (2 Chronicles 6 and 7).
2. Delegating work to your team and trusting that they will also take responsibility of that assignment. This boundary here has been a source of frustration of many leaders that either have trust issues with their team members or find themselves with members who are incompetent or driven by self-agenda. For other leaders it has been a blessing that

speeds up the process to achieving the common goal. A leader with trust issues often projects his insecurity to his team members and has the tendency to want to control performance. Some will consider it micromanaging things and others will call it passion. Regardless of where your opinion stands, this is an unhealthy way of leading and working with others because it ends up irritating and hindering creativity in a team. There are also examples where leaders trusted the work in their team members just to end up disappointed because the motives behind the followers' attachment to the leader were self-driven. They were just waiting for an opportunity to build their own vision on top of the common vision and, in proper time leave, (2 Timothy 4:9–15, 1:15).
3. Nonetheless, delegating work, allows the leader to broaden the scope of his reach and, as said previously, speed up the process to an effective result. In Genesis 1, God was in the midst of creating the world and all that there is; however, on the sixth day, He appointed other people to take over the work He started, so they continued with the momentum. If God was able to delegate then rest on the sixth day, then it is permissible for any leader also to do so.
4. Jesus delegated his followers to continue with the work he started (Matthew 28:18–20). Apostle Paul, one of his followers, continued with the same principle and raised up people able to carry the vision to the extremities of earth while being encouraged to delegate even more people with the same mind-set (2 Timothy 2:2). As MacArthur (2010) explains, delegating betters the organization of the process to the goal. Saying no is often seen as

negative; however, this can be a lifesaving act. Many leaders feel obligated to say yes to every request and sometimes find themselves overwhelmed by the quantity of work because there were no boundaries set over the accountability each group member has over their performance. Researchers believe that leaders that always say yes, even when they cannot, often lack self-confidence and fear that they may be seen as insensible, selfish, and so forth. However, Jesus demonstrated through his life that sometimes no is the best answer to give to some people:

- When the demand is too much to bear at the moment, or the request tries to obstruct previous plans (Luke 5:15–16);
- When facing abuse and skepticism (Luke 4:28–30, 23:8–9);
- When feeling manipulated (Mathew 12:40–50, 16:23);
- When authority, beliefs, and values are being negatively challenged (Luke 4:1–13).

5. Examining for result. This boundary allows for the leader and the team to keep track of the progress they are making and see if there are any changes that need to be applied and not wait to be surprised at the end. According to Friga (2017), this boundary involves documenting expectations and tracking results, it is less about quantitative measures of effectiveness and more about task completion" (32–33). In Genesis 1:31, after completing His task, God self-examined His performance and seemed satisfied by the result. As a leader, you should, at the close of an accomplishment, be able to "see that

it is good." If you fail to establish boundaries around performance and result, you are failing your team and setting yourself up for mediocrity. Examining for result is among the rules of engagement that leads to growth of all the team members.

6. Resting. Again, be reminded to apply healthy boundaries when it comes to your relationship with work. Rest, take a break when needed so you can enjoy the gift that work is to any human being. We have often heard people say, "I will rest in my grave; for now, let me work." Overworking yourself is not a guarantee nor a sign of success. Objective work, however, can lead to it. Resting is not a sign of laziness. It is among the biblical principles of work established by God since the beginning of creation. Rest before your body shuts down on you; rest so you can refresh yourself. (Check Genesis 1 and Acts 20:9.)

7. As a leader, Jesus knew how to establish boundaries for himself. Many leaders would say that successful people never rest or relax, this statement is true in action yet false in effectiveness because science has proven that an exhausted body cannot perform adequately. Also, researchers within the field of leadership have emphasized on the relationship aspect of leadership, thus if we do not have the time to relax, it can become a barrier to our social life and our health.

8. All throughout the four Gospels, there are references to Jesus sleeping, resting, relaxing, and so forth. This, by any means, did not hinder him from fulfilling his vision. Instead, it gave him time to connect with his followers and refresh himself (John 12:2; Mark 6:31–32).

The real purpose of boundaries is to protect the identity of a person as well as the value or belief of the person. In other words, what they believe is right or wrong. In Daniel 3, while many Jews were complying with the general rule of worship established against their God, there is the story of three friends—Shadrach, Meshach, and Abednego—who protected their faith within the parameters of their fear of God. They knew the limit they should never cross and that despite what was offered to them. However, they also understood that there is nothing a man can acquire that can cost more than the truth they know and apply.

In his leadership, most of the time when his beliefs and values were tested, Jesus would refer to the scriptures and begin by saying "It is written" (Matthew 4:1–11 (NIV)) as a way of referring to the book of rules and procedures established.

3) Goods/Wants vs. Boundaries

Temptation hinders you from creating a healthier and godly habit out of your behavior. Temptation comes to shift the focus of your mind to the desire of your flesh so that you ignore the boundaries around the "tree of knowledge of good and evil" in your garden. Your mind-set is a doorway to your perception of things. Pay attention to what you feed your mind with. Learn to differentiate between what you need and what you want. Learn to understand and appreciate times and seasons so that your leadership performance walks in accordance with the revelation of the season in which you are.

Wealth is a great thing. It becomes a problem when it turns into the sole focus of our existence. As a leader, do not chase wealth. Wealth is an added value to the discovered and used gift (Proverbs 18:16). Gehazi failed because in his eyes his greed outweighed his inheritance. Ananias and Saphira failed because their voracity outweighed their partnership with God. Judah failed his loyalty test because of temporary wealth. What destroys people most of the time is the knowledge they didn't have and the knowledge they didn't apply.

Part Four
Conclusion

- There is an intertwined relationship between your faith as a Christian and leadership.
- The scriptures are a reference when it comes to encoding and decoding the art and science of leadership.
- Leadership is a transformative process that produces influence in its environment and the people under the scope of that leadership influence.
- Leadership is service and collaboration to reach the common goal.
- Leadership without an established vision is doomed to confusion.
- Leadership is divinely ordained, and the spiritual, historical, and literary context of the biblical manuscript helps to better understand the concept of such a vast and mysterious subject that is leadership.
- God is the genesis of leadership. Hence, throughout biblical histories and stories, He takes humanity through a journey that unveils ancient secrets concerning leadership, leaders, and followers.
- Mankind is the authorized and established leader over creation. It carries God's features that enables Him to lead over "every and all."
- A believer's mandate as a leader is to oversee, empower, and multiply his kind and his resources.
- Until a person's mind understands and accepts it, leadership will not mean much.
- Leadership realities cannot be avoided; they need to be faced for the leader's mind-set to be transformed.
- A leader's mind-set is the expression of what they nurture in their mind.
- Communication is such a crucial aspect of leadership that God, in Genesis, used it as a channel to bring creation into existence.

- Leadership is a process which outcome depends on how it is handled and approached.
- Leadership is a process which influences and transforms the leader, the followers, and environment in which it flourishes.
- Influence is the currency of leadership.
- Leadership is more than a position; it is the attitude and impact produced.
- Leadership without followers does not exist.
- Leadership might feel lonely, but it is not a journey to loneliness.
- Leadership is serving others while transforming people. It is transforming people through service.
- Leadership is not controlling power; it is empowering others to reach the common goal.
- Leadership is not me; it is us, because common goal always outweighs personal agenda.
- Leadership is vision, vision is mission, and mission is result.
- A vision never dies; it grows or reinvents itself.
- A vision is a present-day explanation of a futuristic idea of how things ought to be.
- Leadership is the ability to rise to responsibility, create, innovate, empower, partner, and delegate.
- Leadership is a relational journey.
- Work is not a chore; it is a divinely established responsibility that requires balance.
- Ethics is every leader's responsibility, and it is at the core of leadership success.
- A leadership built on unethical behaviors and decisions is a failed leadership, and time will tell on it.
- Ethics preservation should be a leader's priority.
- The effectiveness of leadership is in the ability to create and produce a result out of one's work.

- Work ethic is divinely established, but it is each person's responsibility to embrace it.
- Everything that exists today has its spiritual root in God's creative mind.
- God is the ultimate leader.
- The potential to grow the influence of your leadership is hidden in your understanding of "every and all" declared by God in Genesis 1.
- Leadership is in mankind's DNA.
- Your assignment as a leader is to be fruitful, increase, fill, subdue, and rule.
- As a leader, you were divinely appointed and qualified.
- In leadership, relationship is power.
- Do not be afraid to delegate; that is a key to the power of leadership.
- Effective leadership is the ability to multiply its kind.
- Leadership appointment is divine, but leadership elect is human. To appoint is divine; to elect is human.
- Always seek God in your leadership journey.
- Leadership reflects on the heart and mind of a leader.
- Leadership demands taking a leap of faith.
- Leadership consciousness begins in the mind and flows out as a mind-set.
- A leader's niche is often found in what he considers a struggle or a challenge.
- When in doubt, know it is an opportunity to turn to God's leadership and trust Him for guidance.
- Leadership entails discovering and knowing yourself.
- Your imperfection is not your identity.
- Effective leadership flows from the consecration of the right thing.

- When it comes to building a team, quantity never supersedes quality.
- Ambition is the willingness to produce outstanding results.
- There is no leadership without vision.
- Leadership is not easy; neither is it impossible.
- Your ability to communicate will make or break your leadership.
- As much as you care about what you say, pay attention to how you say it, because your non-verbal communicates twice louder.
- As a leader, your vertical communication with God is as important as your horizontal communication with man.
- Strategic leadership is about involving people to create an outcome.
- Communication is the pillar of all forms of interaction in life.
- Gathering people around you is not all there is to building a team.
- Assigning roles and responsibility is a crucial aspect of building a team.

Appendix

A. Self-Reflection Questionnaire

1. How do I define leadership?
2. How do I handle the leadership process I am in?
3. How do I find out the people and territory I am called to as a leader?
4. How can I inspire a shared vision?
5. How do you feel about your leadership role? Does it feel like a God-ordained mandate, or did you accept it because you were elected to the position by census?
6. Can you accept a leadership position even if you do not feel that it is where God calls you?
7. Would you reject a leadership role if you feel inadequate? Even if God calls you to it?
8. As a leader, how would you describe your relationship with God, others, and yourself? Has it changed? Explain your answer.
9. Proverbs 16:3 asks us to commit our work to the Lord to have our plans established. How do you start your workday?
10. How would your dream allow you to fulfill your purposes/mission?
11. Where does your mission come from? Do you think your current strategy will help your vision?
12. Do you think that people will buy into your vision?
13. How do you think God sees you?
14. Apart from your leadership role, who are you and how do you see yourself?
15. Do you think leaders are born or made? Which one would you consider yourself to be?
16. What kind of leader does God want you to be?
17. What virtues define your leadership style?
18. What are some of your innate talents or traits?
19. When you look at your destiny as a leader, what do you see?
20. How comfortable are you about your vision? Does it seem reachable or too big?
21. As Christian leaders, our communication must be vertical and horizontal. How do you personally invest in your vertical and horizontal communication?
22. How effective do you think you are at communication? Would you consider yourself a good communicator?
23. In which area of communication do you think you need more improvement?
24. Is there anyone in your life you consider to be a mentor to you? In which area? How have their contributions impacted you?

B. Must-Know Bible Verses for Leaders

1. **Ephesians 3:16–19 (NIV):** "I pray that out of his glorious riches he may strengthen you with power through his Spirit in your inner being, so that Christ may dwell in your hearts through faith. And I pray that you, being rooted and established in love, may have power, together with all the Lord's holy people, to grasp how wide and long and high and deep is the love of Christ, and to know this love that surpasses knowledge—that you may be filled to the measure of all the fullness of God."
2. **Proverbs 18:21 (NIV):** "The tongue has the power of life and death, and those who love it will eat its fruit."
3. **Proverbs 15:1 (NIV):** "A gentle answer turns away wrath, but a harsh word stirs up anger."
4. **James 3:2 (NLT):** "Indeed, we all make many mistakes. For if we could control our tongues, we would be perfect and could also control ourselves in every other way."
5. **Titus 2:7 (ESV):** "Show yourself in all respects to be a model of good works, and in your teaching show integrity, dignity."
6. **Psalm 16:5–8 (ESV):** "The LORD is my chosen portion and my cup; you hold my lot. The lines have fallen for me in pleasant places; indeed, I have a beautiful inheritance. I bless the LORD who gives me counsel; in the night also, my heart instructs me. I have set the LORD always before me; because he is at my right hand, I shall not be shaken."
7. **Psalm 9:10 (NIV):** "Those who know your name trust in you, for you, Lord, have never forsaken those who seek you."
8. **Ephesians 4:11 (NIV):** "So, Christ himself gave the apostles, the prophets, the evangelists, the pastors and teachers."
9. **1 Corinthians 12:14 (NIV):** "Even so the body is not made up of one part but of many."
10. **Proverbs 3:5–6 (ESV):** "Trust in the LORD with all your heart, and do not lean on your own understanding. In all your ways acknowledge him, and he will make straight your paths."
11. **Psalm 145:14 (ESV):** "The LORD upholds all who are falling and raises up all who are bowed down."
12. **Psalm 139:23–24 (NIV):** "Search me, God, and know my heart; test me and know my anxious thoughts. See if there is any offensive way in me and lead me in the way everlasting."
13. **James 3:16 (NIV):** "For where you have envy and selfish ambition, there you find disorder and every evil practice."
14. **Psalm 147:14 (ESV):** "He makes peace in your borders; he fills you with the finest of the wheat."
15. **Ephesians 4:29 (New American Standard Bible):** "Let no corrupting talk come out of your mouths, but only such as is good for building up, as fits the occasion, that it may give grace to those who hear."

References

Ackermann, Fran, and Colin Eden. *Making Strategy: Mapping Out Strategic Success*. 2nd ed. London: SAGE Publications, 2011.
Adams, William A., and Robert J. Anderson. *Mastering Leadership: An Integrated Framework for Breakthrough Performance and Extraordinary Business Results*. Hoboken, NJ: Wiley, 2016.
Akbar, Hina, Afifa Khanam, Namirah Aslam, Hafiza Gulnaz Fatima, and Noor Muhammad. "Effect of Institutional Culture on the Moral Development of Children." *Journal of Arts & Social Sciences* 2, no. 4 (2017): 71–84.
Alberts, Jess K., Thomas K. Nakayama, and Judith N. Martin. *Human Communication in Society*. Hoboken: Pearson, 2007.
American Bible Society. Good News Bible: Good News Translation. Philadelphia: American Bible Society, 2000.
Anderson, Ryan T. "Virtuous Leadership: An Agenda for Personal Excellence." *First Things: A Monthly Journal of Religion & Public Life*, no. 183 (2008): 62–63.
Andronovienė, Lina. "Leadership as A Virtuous Practice: Reflections on Women and Stained-Glass Ceilings." *Baptistic Theologies* 5, no. 1 (2013): 119–132.
Austin, Wendy, Vangie Bergum, Simon Nuttgens, and Cindy Peternelj-Taylor. "A Re-Visioning of Boundaries in Professional Helping Relationships: Exploring Other Metaphors." *Ethics & Behavior* 16, no. 2 (2006): 77–94.
Baldoni, John. *Great Motivation Secrets of Great Leaders*. New York: McGraw Hill Professional, 2005.
Bazerman, Max H., and Ann E. Tenbrunsel. *Blind Spots: Why We Fail to Do What's Right and What to Do about It*. Princeton: Princeton University Press, 2012.
Bellman, Geoffrey M. *The Consultant's Calling: Bringing Who You Are to What You Do*. Rev ed. San Francisco: Jossey-Bass, 2002.
Berenbeim, Ronald. "Ethical Leadership—Winning with Integrity." *Vital Speeches of The Day* 83, no. 1 (2017): 22–25.
Bible Society New Zealand. NLT Bible: New Living Translation. 2017.
Biech, Elaine. *The Business of Consulting: The Basics and Beyond*. Somerset: Wiley, 2011.
Bishop, William H. "The Role of Ethics in 21st Century Organizations." *Journal of Business Ethics* 118, no. 3 (2013): 635–637.
Block, Peter. *Flawless Consulting: A Guide to Getting Your Expertise Used*. 3rd ed. San Francisco: Jossey-Bass/Pfeiffer, 2011.
Burton, Richard M., Gerardine DeSanctis, and Børge Obel. *Organizational Design: A Step-By-Step Approach*. New York: Cambridge University Press, 2006.
Buzzell, Sid, Bill Perkins, and Kenneth Boa. *Handbook to Leadership: Leadership in the Image of God*. Atlanta: Trinity House Publishers, 2007.
Ciulla, Joanne B., ed. *Ethics: The Heart of Leadership*. 3rd ed. Santa Barbara: Praeger, 2014.

Cloud, Henry. *Boundaries for Leaders: Results, Relationships, and Being Ridiculously in Charge*. New York: Harper Business, 2013.
Cloud, Henry. *Integrity: The Courage to Meet the Demands of Reality*. New York: HarperCollins Publishers, 2006.
Cotroneo, Margartet. "Reflections on Relational Ethics: Toward an Ethic of Revelation." *Journal of Ecumenical Studies* 50, no. 1 (2015): 123–126.
Crossway Bibles. The Holy Bible: English Standard Version. 2003.
Cummings, Thomas G., and Worley, Christopher G. *Organizational Development and Change*. Toronto: Nelson Education, 2010.
Denning, Stephen. *The Secret Language of Leadership: How Leaders Inspire Action through Narrative*. New York: Jossey-Bass, 2007.
DeWitt, David A. *Unraveling the Origins Controversy*. Lynchburg: Creation Curriculum, 2007.
Duvall, J. Scott, and J. Daniel Hays. *Grasping God's Word: A Hands-On Approach to Reading, Interpreting, and Applying the Bible*. Grand Rapids: Zondervan, 2012.
Elm, Griffin. *A First Look at Communication*. New York: McGowan-Hill Humanities/Social Sciences/Languages, 2015.
Engstrom, Ted W. *The Making of a Christian Leader*. Grand Rapids: Zondervan, 1976.
Fackler, Mark, ed. *500 Questions and Answers from the Bible*. Uhrichsville: Barbour, 2006.
Fausset, Andrew R., David Brown, and Robert Jamieson. *Jamieson, Fausset, and Brown's Commentary on the Whole Bible*. Grand Rapids: Zondervan, 1961.
Fedler, Kyle D. *Exploring Christian Ethics: Biblical Foundations for Morality*. Louisville: Westminster John Knox Press, 2006.
Franklin, Robert Michael. *Moral Leadership: Integrity, Courage, Imagination*. Maryknoll: Orbis Books, 2020.
Friga, Paul N. *The McKinsey Engagement: A Powerful Toolkit for More Efficient and Effective Team Problem Solving*. Beijing: Ji Xie Gong Ye Chu Ban She, 2017.
Garrison, Brent. *Leadership by the Book: Lessons from Every Book of the Bible*. Elevate Faith, 2016.
Greenleaf, Robert K. "The Servant as Leader." In the *Servant Leadership: A Journey into the Nature of Legitimate Power and Greatness*, edited by Larry C. Spears. 25th anniversary ed. Mahwah: Paulist Press, 2002.
Gutierrez, Ben. *The Call: Know Personally, Live Passionately*. Bel Air: Academx Publishing Services, 2012.
Hindson, Ed, and Gary Yates, eds. *The Essence of the Old Testament: A Survey*. Nashville: B&H Academic, 2012.
Hodgson, Philip. "Leaders and Managers." *Journal of Occupational Psychology* 58, no. 3 (1985): 260–261, EBSCOhost.
Holy Bible: King James Version Bible. Vereeniging: Christian Art Publishers, 2016.
Holy Bible: New Living Translation. Carol Stream: Tyndale House, 1996.
Hultman, Ken, and Bill Gellermann. *Balancing Individual and Organizational Values: Walking the Tightrope to Success*. San Francisco: Jossey-Bass/Pfeiffer, 2002.
Jennings, Ken, and John Stahl-Wert. *The Serving Leader: Five Powerful Actions to Transform Your Team, Business, and Community*. 10th anniversary ed. Oakland: Berrett-Koehler, 2016.

Jerry, Robert H., II. "Leadership and Followership," Law Review - *The University of Toledo Review* 44, (Winter 2013): 345–354.

Johnson, Craig E., and Michael Z. Hackman. *Leadership: A Communication Perspective*. Long Grove: Waveland Press, 2013.

King James Bible. Nashville: Thomas Nelson, 1991.

Kouzes, James M., and Barry Z. Posner. *A Leader's Legacy*. New York: John Wiley, 2006.

Kouzes, James M., and Barry Z. Posner. *The Leadership Challenge Workbook*. San Francisco: Jossey-Bass, 2004.

Kul, Bekir. "The Impact of Ethical Climate and Ethical Leadership on Ethical Codes Practices." *International Journal of Management Economics & Business/Uluslararasi Yönetim Iktisat Ve Isletme Dergisi* (2017): 563–573.

Lewis, C. S. *Mere Christianity*. New York: Harper Collins Publishers Inc., 1952.

Lingenfelter, Sherwood G. *Leading Cross-Culturally: Covenant Relationships for Effective Christian Leadership*. Grand Rapids: Baker Academic, 2009.

Lomenick, Brad, and Mark Burnett. *H3 Leadership: Be Humble, Stay Hungry, Always Hustle*. Nashville: Nelson Books, an imprint of Thomas Nelson, 2015.

MacArthur, John F. *Called to Lead: 26 Leadership Lessons from the Life of the Apostle Paul*. Nashville: Thomas Nelson, 2010.

Maister, David, Charles H. Green, and Robert M. Galford. *The Trusted Advisor*. New York: Touchstone, 2000.

Maslow, Abraham. *Motivation and Personality*. New York: Harper & Row, 1954.

Maxwell, John C. *The 21 Irrefutable Laws of Leadership: Follow Them and People Will Follow You*. 10th anniversary ed. Nashville: Thomas Nelson, 2007.

Maxwell, John C. *The Maxwell Leadership Bible: New King James Version*. Nashville: Thomas Nelson Bibles, 2018.

Mirsky, Yehudah. "Mixing Prudence with Principle." *New Leader* 76, no. 2 (1993): 20.

Moore, Steve. *The Top 10 Leadership Conversations in the Bible*. Lawrenceville: NexLeader, 2017.

Muehlhoff, Tim, and Todd Lewis. *Authentic Communication: Christian Speech Engaging Culture*. Downers Grove: IVP Academic, 2010.

Northouse, Peter G. *Leadership: Theory and Practice*. 7th ed. Thousand Oaks: SAGE Publications, 2015.

Panait, Cristian. "Emotional Intelligence in Leadership." *Proceedings of The Scientific Conference AFASES* (2017): 2133–2138. doi:10.19062/2247-3173.2017.19.2.18.

Payleitner, Jay. *The 100 Most Important Bible Verses Every Leader Must Know*. Smith Freeman, 2018.

Peng, Wen, and Chen Cheng. "How Does Ethical Leadership Influence Employees' Whistleblowing Intention? Evidence from China." *Social Behavior & Personality: An International Journal* 44, no. 8 (2016): 1255–1266. Doi:10.2224/Sbp.2016.44.8.1255.

Pittarello, Andrea, Margarita Leib, Tom Gordon-Hecker, and Shaul Shalvi. "Justifications Shape Ethical Blind Spots." *Psychological Science* 26, no. 6 (2015): 794–804. https://doi org.ezproxy.regent.edu/10.1177/0956797615571018.

Poulfelt, Flemming, and Thomas H. Olson. *Management Consulting Today and Tomorrow: Perspectives and Advice from Leading Experts*. New York, NY: Routledge, 2018.

Puka, W. "Moral Development." 2005.
http://www.iep.utm.edu/m/moraldev.html.
Randall, Donna M. "Leadership and These of Power: Shaping an Ethical Climate." *The Journal of Applied Christian Leadership* 6, no. 1 (2012): 28–35.
Reagin, Tyler. *The Life-Giving Leader: Learning to Lead from Your Truest Self.* Colorado Springs: WaterBrook, 2018.
Robbins, Vernon K. *Exploring the Texture of Texts: A Guide to Socio-Rhetorical Interpretation.* Valley Forge: Trinity Press International, 1996.
Rothwell, William J. *Effective Succession Planning: Ensuring Leadership Continuity and Building Talent from Within.* New York: American Management Association, 1994.
Samson, Katarzyna. "Trust as a Mechanism of System Justification." *pLoS ONE* 13, no. 10 (2018): 1–22. https://doi-org.ezproxy.regent.edu/10.1371/journal.pone.0205566.
Sanborn, Mark. *The Potential Principle: A Proven System for Closing the Gap Between How Good You Are and How Good You Could Be.* Nashville: Thomas Nelson, 2017.
Scroggins, Clay. *How to Lead When You're Not in Charge: Leveraging Influence When You Lack Authority.* Grand Rapids: Zondervan, 2017.
Shakeel, Fahad, Peter Mathieu Kruyen, and Sandra Van Thiel. "Ethical Leadership as Process: A Conceptual Proposition." *Public Integrity* 21, no. 6 (2019): 613–624. https://doi.org/10.1080/10999922.2019.1606544
Sosik, John. J., and Dongil Jung. *Full Range Leadership Development: Pathways for People, Profit, and Planet.* 2nd ed. New York: Routledge, 2018.
Squires, Susan Elaine. *Inside Arthur Andersen: Shifting Values, Unexpected Consequences.* Upper Saddle River: FT Press, 2003.
Stearns, Richard. *Lead Like It Matters to God: Values-Driven Leadership in A Success-Driven World.* Sydney: Read How You Want, 2021.
Steward, David, and Brandon K. Mann. *Leadership by the Good Book: Timeless Principles for Making An Eternal Impact.* Brentwood: Faithwords, Hachette Book Group, 2020.
Storm, Mark. "Paul and the Reframing of Leadership." *Stimulus: The New Zealand Journal of Christian Thought & Practice* 14, no. 2 (2006): 2–10.
Strock, James. *Serve to Lead 2.0: 21st Century Leaders Manual.* Rev ed. United States: Serve to Lead Group, 2018.
Strong, James. *Strong's Exhaustive Concordance of the Bible.* Peabody: Hendrickson, 2007.
Stubbendorff, Jesper. R., and Robert E. Overstreet. "A Commander's First Challenge: Building Trust." *Air & Space Power Journal* 33, no. 2 (2019): 15–25.
http://search.ebscohost.com.ezproxy.regent.edu:2048/login.aspx?direct=true&db=a9h&N=136668708&site=ehost-live.
The Bible: New International Version. Colorado Springs, CO: International Bible Society, 1984.
The Holy Bible: containing the Old and New Testaments translated out of the original tongues and with the former translations diligently compared & revised. New York: American Bible Society, (986.
Troster, Rabbi Lawrence. "Four Biblical Voices on Our Relationship to Creation." *The Huffington Post.* May 11, 2011.
https://www.huffpost.com/entry/biblical-voices-on-creation_b_859549.

Tuckman, B. W. "Developmental Sequence in Small Groups." *Psychological Bulletin* 63, no. 6 (1965): 384–399. https://doi.org/10.1037/h0022100.

Van Well, Sonja, John P. O'Doherty, and Frans van Winden. "Relief from Incidental Fear Evokes Exuberant Risk-Taking." *pLoS ONE* 14, no. 1 (2019): 1–19. https://doi-org.ezproxy.regent.edu/10.1371/journal.pone.0211018.

Verderber, Kathleen S., Rudolph F. Verderber, and Deanna D. Sellnow. *Communicate!* Boston: Wadsworth/Cengage Learning, 2017.

Waite, Maurice. "Influence." In *Pocket Oxford English Dictionary.* 11th ed. Oxford: Oxford University Press, 2013.

Weiss, Alan, and Omar Khan. *The Global Consultant: How to Make Seven Figures Across Borders.* Singapore: John Wiley and Sons , 2009.

Weymouth, Richard. The Holy Bible: Weymouth New Testament. Low Tide Press Edition, 2017.

Witherington, Ben, III. *Work: A Kingdom Perspective on Labor.* Paju: Neus Cross, 2016.

Woolfe, Lorin. *Bible on Leadership: From Moses to Matthew—Management Lessons for Contemporary Leaders.* New York: Amacom, 2019.

Wright, N. T. *After You Believe: Why Christian Character Matters.* New York: Harper Collins, 2012.

Acknowledgments

Thinking about writing this manuscript was one thing; actually writing it was another. I did not know it would demand a lot from me in all aspects of my life. I wish I could mention the plethora of people who, in one way or another, are supporting me in this journey. However, wherever they are, they should know that my gratitude and prayer for them will never cease. This book is not my work alone. It is our work, and we have all, in one way or another, coauthored this oeuvre.

Thank you especially to:

- The love of my life, Francis D. Mangala, and our children
- The Toto Furume Family: Iris, Israel, Irman, Iselle, Isaac, Igra, Iryelle, and Ibertine. Thank you for being the ground upon which my leadership was tested.
- My parents, Toto Furume and Elodie Katumbo M. Not only have you exemplified leadership in my sight but thank you for making sure everything was gathered for me to excel in my destiny.
- Mangala, Furume, Adounkpe, J. Kabolete Family
- Dr. Kibby Otoo
- Rev. Schekinah Masudi
- Rev. Joel Francis Tatu
- Ezekiel 37 Mission

And finally, my Lord and Savior, Jesus Christ.
Thank you.

About the Author

Dr. Ines Furume-Mangala is an author, speaker, ordained minister of the Gospel, an entrepreneur, a philanthropist, and a doctor in strategic leadership. She has traveled all around the globe as an evangelical missionary and a public speaker, sharing the message of hope, empowerment, and restoration.

Ines is a strategic communication and leadership consultant specializing in global leadership, professional and speech communication. She has served as lead visionary and president of Ezekiel 37 Mission and House of Imani Foundation for several years now.

Follow her on social media @inesfurume
Check out her website: www.ezekiel37mission.org

www.ingramcontent.com/pod-product-compliance
Lightning Source LLC
Chambersburg PA
CBHW071858070526
44583CB00016B/1745